D1197178

THE ELEMENTS OF
SOCIAL SCIENTIFIC
THINKING

THE ELEMENTS OF SOCIAL SCIENTIFIC THINKING ♦♦♦♦♦

KENNETH R. HOOVER
The College of Wooster

St. Martin's Press   New York

Library of Congress Catalog Card Number: 75–33511
Copyright © 1976 by St. Martin's Press, Inc.
All Rights Reserved.
Manufactured in the United States of America.
09876
fedcba
For information, write: St. Martin's Press, Inc.,
175 Fifth Avenue, New York, N. Y. 10010

Book design by Margaret Dodd.

Cover painting: The Solomon R. Guggenheim Museum, New York,
Laszlo Moholy-Nagy: AII, 1924.

For
Lee Armstrong Hoover and Margaret Whitcomb Hoover
with memories of wisdom and love

PREFACE

This little book is not very complicated. It is, rather, an
initiation to social science intended both for those who
need to know how to evaluate the results of social science
and for those who are taking their first steps as researchers.
Where do concepts come from? What is a variable? Why
bother with scientific thinking? How is a hypothesis different from other sentences about reality; how is it similar?
These and other fundamental queries are dealt with here.
The operational advice on research is elaborated only as

far as is required to gain a foothold on understanding scientific inquiry. Throughout, the emphasis is on reality-testing as the process by which we can know what to make of the world. The presentation of science is not parochial —I encourage the reader to be scientific in the general sense of daily thought as well as in the specific application of social scientific method.

There are various points of access to the book depending upon the reader's needs. The first chapter, "Thinking Scientifically," sets social science in the general context of the various ways people try to answer questions about the world around them. Chapter Two, "The Elements of Science," develops the basic outline of the scientific method by discussing concepts, variables, measurements, and hypotheses. For those faced with the immediate task of doing or understanding research, Chapter Three, entitled "Strategies," may be a good point of entry since it deals more directly with the nuts and bolts of scientific inquiry. Chapter Four, "Refinements," presumes a basic understanding of the scientific method and supplies a more extensive repertory of tools for research. The final chapter, "Reflections: Back to the Roots," should be read, I think, by those who use the book for whatever purpose. The point of the concluding chapter is to place scientific understanding in perspective and to suggest generally where humility is necessary and achievement possible.

For convenience of access and review, each chapter begins with an outline of the topics covered and ends with the major concepts introduced listed in the general order of their appearance.

In the Appendix, an article by Professor Lewis Lipsitz of the University of North Carolina, "Work Life and Political Attitudes," is reprinted. The article is cited frequently in the text. Those who wish to have a good model for the design and discussion of a research project may want to consider it carefully. I appreciate the permission of the *American Political Science Review* and Professor Lipsitz to reprint the article, which originally appeared in the *APSR* 58 (December 1964): 951–962. My thanks also for permission to use the cartoon by "Lorenz" that appeared in the December 9, 1974, issue of *The New Yorker*, and to Newsweek, Inc. and Simon and Schuster, Inc., for permission to reprint Table 4.1 in Chapter Four.

A liberal arts college can be a good place to write a book like this; there is an easily accessible community of scholars in the various disciplines of social science. My list of acknowledgments thus includes some especially helpful colleagues. Bob Blair was a good friend and trusty resource throughout the project. Philip Zweifel's scrutiny of the manuscript rescued the syntax in places, Gene Pollock helped illuminate a few statistical mysteries, Frank Miller and Steve Victor aided in making substantive some random ruminations. In addition to Frank Miller, Bradlee Karan and Gordon Shull contributed suggestions to an earlier form of the first two chapters written with the support of an NSF-COSIP grant to the Department of Political Science. My Senior Thesis students and those in American Politics and Empirical Theory were valued, though unwitting, accomplices in refining these ideas, as were the participants in the Social Science Roundtable. The College of Wooster leave program and Faculty Development Fund supplied essential support for which I am grateful.

Aage Clausen of Ohio State University did a particularly thoughtful and meticulous critique of the manuscript. Working with Barry Rossinoff, Executive Editor for St. Martin's Press, was a pleasure. I appreciate very much his confidence in this effort and the guidance of the anonymous critics he selected.

To all of these I am indebted, as are the readers of this book, though neither they nor I may hold them responsible for the result.

Judy Hoover contributed some helpful suggestions in the writing, and a lot more that this husband couldn't begin to acknowledge. Andrew and Erin appear briefly in the second chapter and are present throughout in the nurture of the spirit they provide to their father.

KENNETH R. HOOVER
The College of Wooster

CONTENTS

CONTENTS

THE ELEMENTS OF
SOCIAL SCIENTIFIC
THINKING

OUTLINE

CHAPTER ONE

THINKING SCIENTIFICALLY

"Science searches the common experience of people; and it is made by people, and it has their style."

JACOB BRONOWSKI

"Social science" in cold print gives rise to images of some robot in a statistics laboratory reducing human activity to bloodless digits and simplified formulas. Research reports filled with mechanical-sounding words like "empirical," "quantitative," "operational," "inverse," and "correlative" aren't very poetic. Yet the stereotypes of social science created by these images are, I will try to show, wrong.

Like any other mode of knowing, social science can be used for perverse ends; however, it can also be used for humane personal understanding. By testing thoughts against reality, science helps to liberate inquiry from bias, prejudice, and just plain muddleheadedness. So it is unwise to be put off by simple stereotypes—too many people accept these stereotypes and deny to themselves the power of social scientific understanding.

The word "science" stands for a very great deal in our culture—some even consider it the successor to religion in the modern age. Our object here is to find a path into the scientific mode of inquiry, not to examine the whole range of issues associated with science. In order to find that path, we will begin not by defining science, but rather by allowing science to emerge out of contrasts with other forms of knowledge.

First, we have to identify some distractions that should be ignored. Science is sometimes confused with technology, which is the application of science to various tasks. Grade school texts that caption pictures of rockets on the moon with the title, "Science Marches On!" aid such confusion. The technology that makes landings on the moon possible emerged from the use of scientific strategies in the study of propulsion, electronics, and numerous other fields. It is the mode of inquiry that is scientific; the rocket is a piece of technology.

Just as science is not technology, neither is it some specific body of knowledge. The popular phrase "*Science tells us* [for example] that smoking is bad for your health" really misleads. "Science" doesn't tell us anything; people tell us things, in this case people who have used scientific strategies to investigate the relationship of smoking to health. Science, as a way of thought and investigation, is best conceived of as existing not in books, or in machinery, or in reports containing numbers, but rather in that invisible world of the mind. Science has to do with the way questions are formulated and answered; science is a set of rules and forms for inquiry created by people who want reliable answers.

Another distraction comes from identifying particular persons as "scientists." That usage is not erroneous, since presumably the people so labeled are committed to the scientific form of inquiry, but neither is it fully honest to say that some people are scientists, whereas others are presumably nonscientists. Science is a mode of inquiry that, we will see shortly, is common to all human beings. Some people specialize in scientific approaches to knowledge, but we are all participants in the scientific way of thinking.

In becoming more self-conscious of your own habits of thought, you will find that there is some science in all of us. We measure, compare, modify beliefs, and acquire a kind of savvy about evidence in the daily business of figuring out what to do next and how to relate to others. The simplest of games involves the testing of tactics and strategies against the data of performance, and that is crudely scientific. Even trying out different styles of dress for their impact on others has an element of science in it.

The scientific way of thought is one of a number of strategies by which we try to cope with a vital reality: the uncertainty of life. We don't know what the consequences of many of our actions will be. We may have little idea of the forces that affect us subtly or directly, gradually or suddenly. In trying to accomplish even the simplest task, like figuring out what to eat, we do elementary calculations of what might taste good or what might be good for us. If there's enough uncertainty on that score, a little advance testing is a good idea: the king has his taster, and the rest of us, at least when it comes to a certain hamburger, have the assurance that billions have already been sold.

The scientific approach has many competitors in the search for understanding. For many people during most of history, the competition has prevailed. Analysis of reality has usually been much less popular than myths, superstitions, and hunches, which have the reassuring feel of certainty *before* the event they try to predict or control, though seldom afterwards. People starve every day because of their refusal to eat good food that is believed to be sacred or thought to be polluting. Personal beliefs do have their place. Sometimes unverified belief sponsors an inspired action or sustains the doubtful to a better day. The point merely is that the refusal to analyze is crippling, and the skilled analyst is in a position of strength.

Why Bother to Be Systematic?

Most human communication takes place among small groups of persons who share a common language and much common experience and understanding of the world they live in. There is a ready-made arena for mutual agreement or argument. Not so in a more complex social environment. Though families can transmit wisdom across generations by handing down stories and maxims, societies run into trouble. In its most cynical form, the question is, "Whose myth is to be believed?" The necessities of communication, let alone the need for personal understanding of the environment, generate a need for systematic thought and inquiry. Because society is interesting for the drama it contains, there is a tendency to dispense with systematic understanding and get on with the descriptions, stories, and personal judgments. These can be illuminating, though they often have limited usefulness because highly subjective accounts of life form a poor basis for the formation of common understanding and common action.

The intricate task of getting people to bridge the differences that arise from the particularity of their experience requires a more disciplined approach to knowledge. *Knowledge is socially powerful only if it is knowledge that can be put to use.* Social knowledge, if it is to be useful, must be both *transmissible* and *valid*. In order to be transmissible, knowledge must be in clear form. And if the knowledge is intended to be used as a spur to action, it must be convincing enough to create an impulse to action in the audience. A statement such as, "I think that capitalism exploits the poor," may influence one's friends and even relatives to think that there is some injustice in our society. But it probably won't make any waves with others. If, however, you can cite the evidence that, "In our capitalistic system, 10 percent of the people control 50 percent of the wealth, and 50 percent of the people control less than 10 percent of the wealth," a more compelling argument results because you relate a judgment to a measurement of reality. People who don't even like you, but who favor some kind of fairness in wealth distribution, might find such a statement a powerful cue to examine our economic system critically. Knowledge built on evidence, and captured in clear transmissible form, makes for power over the environment.

Accumulating knowledge so that past mistakes can be avoided has always intrigued civilized humanity. One can record the sayings of wise persons, and that does contribute greatly to cultural enrichment. Yet there is surely room for another kind of cumulative effort: the building up of statements evidenced in a manner that can be double-checked by others. To double-check a statement requires that one know precisely what was claimed and how the claim was tested. This is a major part of the enterprise of science. The steps to be discussed in the ensuing section on "The Ingredients of a Scientific Strategy" are the guideposts for accomplishing that kind of knowing.

Reasoned Judgment and Opinion

All this vaguely ominous talk about systematic thinking is not meant to cast out reasoned judgment, opinion, and imagination. There is no particular sense in limiting the facilities of the mind in any inquiry.

Reasoned judgment is a staple of human understanding. A reasoned judgment bears a respectable relationship to evidence. Because people inevitably have to act in the absence of complete evidence for decision-making, the term "judgment" is important. Judgment connotes decision-making in which all the powers of the mind are activated to make the best use of available knowledge.

Reasoned judgment is the first part of systematic thought. The proposition that, "A full moon on the eve of election day promotes liberal voting," could be correct, but it does not reflect much reasoned judgment since there is neither evidence for linking the two events nor a logical connection between them. An investigator with time and resources might look into such a proposition, but in a world of scarce time, inadequate resources, and serious problems of social analysis to engage rare talents, such an investigation makes little sense.[1] Although the proposition may be intuitive, even intuition usually bears some relationship to experience and evidence.

Opinion likewise plays an inescapable role in scientific analysis, because all efforts at inquiry proceed from some personal interest or other. No one takes himself or herself off dead center to ask a question unless he or she has an interest in what the conclusion might be. Furthermore, each person's angle of vision on reality is necessarily slightly different from the angle of another. Opinion can't be eliminated from inquiry, but it can be controlled so that it does not fly off into complete fantasy. One practice that assists in reducing the role of opinion is for the researcher to be self-conscious of his or her values and opinions.

Plato's famous aphorism, "Know thyself," applies here more than ever. Much damage has been done to the cause of good social science by those who pretend disinterest to the point where their research conceals opinions that covertly structure their conclusions. No one is truly objective, certainly not about the nature of society—there are too many personal stakes involved for that.

---

[1] However, police and bartenders will tell you that the night of a full moon does in fact bring out some pretty bizarre behavior; the hypothesis isn't completely preposterous.

Ultimately, good science provides its own check on the influence of values in an inquiry. If the method by which the study has been done and the evidence for conclusions are clearly and fully stated, the study can be examined for the fit of conclusions to evidence. If there is doubt about the validity of what has been done, the study itself can be double-checked, or "replicated," to use the technical term. This feature distinguishes science from personal judgment. No one can double-check everything that goes on as the mind deals with inner feelings, perceptions of experience, and thought processes. Science brings the steps of inquiry out of the mind and into public view so they can be shared as part of the process of accumulating knowledge.

Imagination, Custom, and Intuition

The mind, in its many ways of knowing, is never so clever or so mysterious as in the exercise of *imagination*. If there is any sense in which people can leap over tall obstacles at a single bound, it is in the flight of the mind. But it is one thing to imagine a possible proposition about reality, and it is quite another to start imagining evidence.

Science is really a matter of figuring out relationships between things we know something about. To propose a relationship is a creative and imaginative act, however much systematic preparation may lie in the background. To test a proposition against reality involves a different order of imagination—mainly the ability to find in the bits and pieces of information elicited from reality that item essential to testing the credibility of a particular idea.

It is in the realm of discovery that science becomes

a direct partner of imagination. The history of natural science is filled with examples, from the realization that the earth revolves around the sun, and not vice versa, to the discovery that matter is made up of tiny atoms. Each of these discoveries was made by bold and imaginative people who were not afraid to challenge a whole structure of customary belief by consulting evidence in the real world. While these were discoveries on the grand scale, the same sort of effort is involved in stepping outside accepted explanations of human behavior to imagine other possibilities and test them by the intelligent use of evidence. To be truly imaginative is something like trying to escape gravity—the initial move is the hardest. While the social sciences have as yet few discoveries to compare with the feats of natural science, the application of science to social relations is a much more recent and vastly more complicated undertaking.[2]

Whatever we may come to say about the careful thinking scientific analysis requires, there is still no way to capture completely the wondrous process of "having

[2] Perhaps one of the earliest attempts to confront social custom with science was the effort in the late nineteenth century by Francis Galton, an English scientist, to test the efficacy of prayer. Observing that prayers were daily offered in churches throughout the land for the long life of royalty, he compared their longevity to that of the gentry and a variety of professionals. He found, after excluding deaths by accident or violence, and including only those who had survived their thirtieth year, that the average age of decease for royalty was 64.04 years, the lowest age for all his categories. Galton did observe, however, that prayer has many personal uses aside from the fulfillment of requests. And, who knows, royalty might have died even sooner but for such petitions. P. B. Medawar, *Induction and Intuition in Scientific Thought* (Philadelphia: American Philosophical Society, 1969), pp. 2–7.

an idea." Science is absolutely *not* a system for frustrating that exercise of intuition and imagination; rather, it is a set of procedures for making such ideas as fruitful and productive as human ingenuity allows. Even the most wonderful idea, whatever its source, is only as good as its relationship to some present or potential reality. Science is the art of reality-testing, of taking ideas and confronting them with evidence drawn from the phenomena to which they relate.

To step back from the general blur of human relationships and to envision alternative possibilities demands a level of imagination that is as uncommon as it is necessary. In the usual run of social and political experience, David Hume's observation may be sadly accurate: "Men, once accustomed to obedience, never think of departing from that path in which they and their ancestors trod and to which they are confined by so many urgent and visible motives." [3] Yet it is in the understanding and reform of social and political arrangements that the world requires the very best application of disciplined imagination. That the world we live in is unsatisfactory in these respects is evidenced by the amount of time spent drilling into the heads of the young patriotic slogans and altruistic maxims that bear little relationship to the reality of the state or the frequency of human benevolence. If our community life could be made more sensible and humane, these rituals would not require so much effort. In the absence of imaginative efforts to understand the reality of society, we are

[3] "Of the Origin of Government," *Political Essays*, ed. Charles Hendel (New York: Liberal Arts Press, 1953), p. 41.

confined to the beaten path of custom and the inequities that stifle human potential.

Custom is not all bad, for it may embody the lessons learned from a long, often unhappy, experience with reality and is, in a vague way, scientific. Custom frequently holds communities together in the face of enormous and even violent pressures. Yet the task of any social science must be to understand why things are the way they are, as well as how the elements of social life can be reformed to allow for more humane patterns of personal development and expression. The weapons in this struggle for understanding are not only science with its procedures for disciplining inquiry, but also the intuition that life can be better than it is, that a given pattern of behavior may be other than inevitable, that even the smallest transactions of behavior may contain keys to larger structures of possibility and potential.

The method of any effort at understanding involves a tension between thought and investigation. There are various ways of linking these two components. The mystic perceives an inner truth and interprets "signs" he or she finds in reality as symptoms of the validity of his or her insight. The historian looks for patterns in the past and, having conceptualized them, suggests their usefulness in interpreting the major features of previous events. Thus the "rise of the middle class" in Europe becomes a major interpretive concept. Someone who is scientific attempts to be more precise than the mystic or the historian with respect to the *thoughts* by which research is guided, the *data* regarded as significant in the investigation, and the *measures* used in testing mental constructions against reality.

13

CONCEPTS INTRODUCED

Science	Opinion
Technology	Objectivity
Transmissible knowledge	Imagination
Valid knowledge	Custom
Reasoned judgment	Intuition

OUTLINE

CHAPTER TWO

THE ELEMENTS
OF SCIENCE

"[Scientific inquiry] begins as a story about a Possible World—a story which we invent and criticize and modify as we go along, so that it ends by being, as nearly as we can make it, a story about real life."

P. B. MEDAWAR

The building blocks of a scientific strategy are, in themselves, simple to understand. They are: concepts, variables, hypotheses, and measurements. The way in which these are combined constitutes the scientific method. First, we will try to put each block in place.

Concepts

If you had to purge all words and other symbols from your mind and confront the world with a virgin mind, what would you do? Without a body to sustain, you might do nothing. The necessities of survival, however, start closing in, and the first act of the mind might be to sort out the edible objects from the inedible, then the warm from the cold, the friendly from the hostile. From there it isn't very far to forming concepts like food, shelter, warmth, and symbolizing these concepts in the form of words or utterances. Thus, humbly, emerges the instrument called language. The search for truly usable concepts and categories is under way. Languages are nothing more than huge collections of names for things, feelings, and ideas.

Some concepts and classifications might not be very helpful. To conceptualize all plants under only a single designation would preclude further distinctions between those to be eaten, those that heal, and those that poison. Some concepts relate to experience too vaguely: English has but one word for something so various and complicated as love. Greek allows three concepts: *eros* for romantic love, *agape* for generalized feelings of affection, and *filios* for family love. The weakness of English in dealing with love affects everyone's experience through the tricky ways the word is used in our culture.

Notice that reality-testing is built right into the process of naming things, one of the most elementary transactions of existence. That back-and-forth between the stimuli of the environment and the reflections of the mind makes up the kind of thought we will be trying to capture for analysis.

After several thousand years of history, we still have to face the fact that the process of naming things is difficult. Language emerges essentially by agreement. You and I and the other members of the family (tribe, state, nation, world) agree, for example, to call things that twinkle in the sky "stars." Unfortunately these agreements may not be very precise. In common usage, the term "star" covers a multitude of objects, big and small, hot and cold, solid and gaseous.

To call a thing by a precise name is the beginning of understanding, because it is the key to the procedure that allows the mind to grasp reality and its many relationships. It makes a great deal of difference whether an illness is conceived of as caused by the Evil Spirit or by bacteria on a binge. The concept *bacteria* is tied to a system of concepts in which there is a connection to a powerful repertory of treatments, that is, antibiotics.

Movie serials about jungle tribes and Indians often have an episode featuring a confrontation between the local medicine man and the doctor who triumphs for modern science by saving the chief or his child. The cultural agreement that supported the medicine man is shattered by the scientist with his microscope. Sadly for the children of modern medicine, it turns out there were a few tricks in the medicine man's bag that were ignored or lost in the euphoria of such a "victory" for science. Even less happy was the arrogance with which many of the cultural agreements expressed in native languages were undermined through the supposition of superiority by conquering powers. To capture meaning in a language is a profound and subtle process, even if it is a little sloppy. While you are invited to be precise about concepts, you are not invited to be arrogant about the utility of your new knowledge for reworking lives, societies, and civilizations.

The importance of having the right name for a thing can hardly be overestimated. Thomas Hobbes, a seventeenth-century political theorist, thought the proper naming of things so important to the establishment of political order that he made this a central function of the sovereign. King James understood the message and ordered an authoritative translation of the Bible as a way of overcoming violent squabbles about the precise meanings of words in the Scripture. More to the modern scene, George Orwell, in his antiutopian novel, 1984, gave us a vision of a whole bureaucracy devoted to reconstructing language concepts to enhance the power of a totalitarian society. A recent presidential press secretary made a game try at redefining "lie" by calling a previous statement "inoperative." These examples are intended to make you aware that, by tinkering with the meanings of concepts, you are playing with the foundations of human understanding and social control.

But it will be a while before you master the scientific method sufficiently to pull off anything very grand. For now, the point is that concepts are: (1) tentative, (2) based on agreement, and (3) useful only to the degree that they capture or isolate some significant and definable item in reality.

What have concepts got to do with science? If you've spent any time around babies, you may notice they often try to show off by pointing at things and naming them. It gets a little boring the tenth or fifteenth time through, but babies take justifiable pride in the exercise. Next come sentences. From naming things, from being able to symbolize something rather than simply pointing at it, comes the next step in moving reality around so it can produce things that are needed. The first sentence our son, Andrew, spoke was to his sister, Erin. Sitting on a little cart he said, "Erin, push me!" She did.

What you are reading now is an effort to link together concepts to expand your understanding. People speak sentences by the thousands in an attempt to move reality into some useful response. Most of them don't have the good luck Andrew did on his first try. Often the concepts are confusing, and the connections are vague or unlikely, not to mention the problem the speaker has with the listener's perceptions and motives.

Thought develops through the linking of concepts. Consider, as an example, Pierre Proudhon's famous proposition, "Property is theft!" Property, as a concept, stands for the notion that a person can claim sole ownership of land or other resources. Theft, of course, means the act of taking something without justification. By linking these two concepts through the verb "is," Proudhon meant to equate the institution of private property with the denial of humankind's common ownership of nature's resources. The concept of privately owned property was, he thought, unjustifiable thievery. While Proudhon's declaration illustrates the linkage of concepts at the lofty philosophical level, the humblest sentence performs the same operation.

Science is a way of checking on the formulation of concepts and testing the possible linkages between them through references to observable phenomena. The next step is to see how scientists use a special kind of concept, the *variable,* to form a special kind of sentence, the *hypothesis.*

21

Variables

A variable is a name for something that is thought to influence a particular state of being in something else. Heat is one variable in making water boil, and so is pressure. Age has been established as a modestly important variable in voting; however, there are many other more significant variables: socioeconomic standing, parental influence, race, sex, region of residence, and so on.

A variable is, in addition, a special kind of concept that contains within it a notion of degree or differentiation. Temperature is an easily understood example of a variable. It includes the notion of more or less heat. Religion is a variable of a different kind; though there may be such a thing as more or less religion, it is likely that one would look to the several denominations of religion in, for example, assessing voting behavior. In 1968, the Gallup Poll found that a fairly predictable 35 percent of Protestants voted Democratic for president, but an abnormally low 59 percent of Catholics voted for the Democrats' Humphrey. This signaled a defection from the Kennedy-Johnson years when the Catholic percentages were in the high 70s. Evidence such as this permits us to say something intelligent about the relationship between two variables: religion and voting.

While most variables deal with differences of degree, as in temperature, or differences of variety, like religion, some variables are even simpler. These deal with the most elementary kind of variation: present or absent, there or not there, existent or nonexistent. Take pregnancy, for example. There is no such thing as a little bit of it. Either the condition exists or it doesn't.

Variable definition, dull as it may seem, is a very creative process and often raises immense questions. Consider, as an illustration, such an ordinary variable as time. The early Greeks puzzled a good deal over how to conceptualize this variable. It seems obvious that time has to be thought of as having a beginning—so philosophers went about trying to figure out when the beginning was. Yet the nagging question always popped up—What happened before that? Plato and Aristotle both played with the idea that time might not be linear at all, that is, it might *not* have a beginning, a progression, and presumably an end. It just might be cyclical! This seems crazy to us children of linear time, but they were thinking that universal time might be something like the cycle of the body, a rhythm found everywhere in nature. Historic time, therefore, might best be conceived of as an unfolding structure of events in which one follows the other until the whole pattern is played out and the entire cycle starts over again. Aristotle commented that it just might be that he himself "was living *before* the Fall of Troy quite as much as *after* it; since, when the wheel of fortune had turned through another cycle, the Trojan War would be re-enacted and Troy would fall again." [1]

The social science done by introductory students seldom involves such mind-boggling conceptual problems, yet it wouldn't do to pretend these problems don't exist. The variable *personality*, for example, is reputed to have

---

[1] Stephen Toulmin and June Goodfield, *The Discovery of Time* (New York: Harper & Row, 1965), p. 46.

over four hundred definitions in the professional literature, partly because personality is a compound of a huge range of other variables: class, status, self-concept, race, socialization, and so forth. The complexity of personality as a variable has driven social scientists to such awkward definitions as: "One's acquired, relatively enduring, yet dynamic, unique system of predispositions to psychological and social behavior."[2] Even when social scientists agree on the description of a variable, that doesn't mean the definition possesses the qualities of eternal truth—it just means that some people who have thought about it carefully agree that a given definition seems to help answer some questions. This is frustrating, but that's all that can be said, except to point out that *not* facing the problem of specifying variables in analysis doesn't make the problem go away, it just gets you further into the linguistic soup.

The huge stock of concepts in language creates enormous possibilities for linking up variables to explain events. People have muddled around for centuries trying to sort through significant connections. Science is a slightly elevated form of muddling by which these connections are tried out and tested as carefully as possible. In medical science, it took centuries to isolate the many variables affecting disease. Only recently has medical science become so disciplined that it can diagnose many diseases through highly significant blood-chemistry analysis. This development represents the present stage of a long process of isolating and eliminating a host of unimportant or marginally significant variables. Western doctors have just

[2] Gordon DiRenzo, *Personality and Politics* (Garden City, N.Y.: Anchor Books, 1974), p. 16.

recently come up against an ancient form of medicine developed to a high art in China, and now we have medical scientists scrambling to figure out why acupuncture works. Whole new sets of variables must now be considered and new conceptual bridges built.

Unfortunately for *social* science, we have barely figured out how to lay the foundation for a structure of theory to explain social behavior. Many new students of social science do not see—especially when confronted by fat texts in introductory courses—the context of struggle and accomplishment, tentativeness and probability, behind what has been achieved in social understanding.

Social science currently contains many subdivisions (e.g., political science, sociology, economics, psychology), all of which are working on specific variables within subsystems of behavior. Social scientists are in the process of chasing a good many possible connections between variables. The bits of tested knowledge that do emerge await an integration across the lines of these inquiries. Relatively few have been attempted, though these efforts are bound to increase in view of the dramatic need for comprehensive social understanding.

Quantification and Measurement: How to Get Inside a Variable

We said earlier that variables are special concepts that contain within them some notion of degree or differentiation. The next question is: How does one pin down that degree or differentiation? The answer involves a two-step process: quantification and measurement.

The idea of *quantification* means setting up a standard

amount of a thing and putting a label on it. The origins of some quantifications are pretty weird. The English, for example, needed a standard quantity of distance, so they settled on the length of some king's foot. For a long time, the foot competed with the cubit, which was the length of someone else's forearm. The trouble with the cubit was that they could never agree on what the standard forearm was—some said seventeen inches, some said twenty-one inches. Consequently, we don't hear much about cubits anymore.

Isolating standardized units increases the power of description and analysis. When Gabriel Fahrenheit established the idea of a degree of temperature, he made possible a much more useful description of hot and cold. It makes a considerable difference with respect to a puddle of water if the temperature is thirty-two degrees rather than thirty-three degrees—the word "cold" doesn't work very well for capturing that vital degree of difference.

Quantification in social science takes two forms: discrete and continuous. Discrete quantification relates to counting the units of a thing. A vote is a discrete and specific act that can be counted in a conventional manner. Some quantifications, however, have to capture the notion of variation along a continuum. Age is an example of a continuous quantification. True, one can count the number of years in a person's age, but the quantification of age is an expression of something that is ongoing. I am 35.123 years old today, next Monday I will be 35.142 years old. Continuous quantification deals not with discrete items, but rather with dimensions such as age, length, and time. The mark of continuous quantification is that the variable involved may have any value on a scale, whereas in discrete quantification only whole numbers appear, as in a counting process.

Each variable has its own peculiar problems and potentials for quantification. One of the distinguishing characteristics of a well-developed science is the array of useful quantifiable variables it has developed; one of the marks of a smart scientist is the ability to find ways of quantifying important variables in a reliable and meaningful way. Economics has come a long way by using money as a unit of analysis. Many powerful economic indicators, such as the gross national product or the consumer price index, are based on money. Unfortunately for the other social sciences, there aren't such easily quantifiable units for psychological stress, alienation, happiness, personal security, and so on. Yet inventive scientists have found more or less successful ways of capturing quantifiable pieces of these variables. A text in any of these areas contains dozens of illustrations, and we will see some of them in the next chapter. The importance of quantification is that, when it can be accomplished, there is the potential for more precise measurement.

Measurement is not something we choose to do or not do—it is inherent in every analytic discussion. If you doubt this, listen carefully in the next conversation you have and notice your dependence on terms that imply measurement. A simple political statement such as, "Democrats generally favor the poor," involves measurement. The verb "favor" implies degrees of difference, and so does the term "poor." The modifier "generally" is an attempt to qualify the measurement by indicating that it is not a universal characteristic of the attitudes of all Democrats.

If quantities can be established, measurement becomes much easier. The most obvious measurement deals with the problem of *how much*. How much distance, how much money, and so forth. Some questions of how much are not so easy to measure; public opinion, for example. Using responses to questions as the quantifiable unit of analysis, the most elementary technique divides opinion into favorable versus unfavorable. "Are you for it or against it?" Public opinion polling is usually done on this basis. One thing such a simple measurement conceals, of course, is the intensity of the opinion. On many political issues there may be minorities who are passionately on one side and a majority that is lukewarmly on the other side. Some public opinion polls deal with this by using four categories instead of two:

Strongly For   For   Against   Strongly Against

An even fancier way of addressing the problem is to use scales: a scale of 1 to 10, from never-say-die opposition to enthusiastic support. This helps expand the range of responses and reveals more accurately the state of opinion. A political system that simply acts on majority sentiment without taking intensity into account can get itself into a lot of trouble—as this nation did on the Vietnam War. A passionate minority of opponents became embittered and alienated by the reliance of policy makers on a rather unenthusiastic majority of supporters.

Measurement, properly conceived and executed, at least has the potential for reducing the ambiguity of words and sentences. At the same time, improperly conceived measurement is dangerous precisely because it can be so powerful. A tragic and repugnant example is the use of "body counts" as a key to "progress" in the U.S. effort in Vietnam. There were two things wrong with this quantified measurement. First, it didn't measure what some policy makers alleged that it measured: the amount of success or failure in achieving overall objectives in the war. Since the war was at least as much a political and psychological struggle as a military conflict, the body counts were worse than useless as an index of success. They may have told the military something about the condition of the enemy, but reliance on them promoted adverse political and psychological effects in the Vietnamese population and in ours—to say nothing of the morality involved.

A second flaw in the measurement was its implementation. Troops in the field were supposed to count enemy dead and report the number. However, several factors intervened: the confusion (sometimes deliberate) about who was the enemy, the error introduced by having more than one person counting in a particular location, and the chain-of-command pressures for a high body count. Consequently, while the body counts kept going up and led to predictions of success in the war, the actual situation deteriorated.[3]

The very important point is that sloppy or inappropriate measurement is generally worse than no measurement at all. Interpreting the results of measurement requires an understanding of the measurement itself.

---

[3] Body-counting as an indicator reached immoral depths with "bounty-hunting" in which U.S. Army counter-intelligence units hired assassins to kill suspected communist sympathizers—the payments were made by the number of *ears* brought in to headquarters. Where money was involved, the counting was made more specific. Michael Drosnin, *New Times Magazine* 5 (22 August 1975): 16–24.

The Hypothesis

Although much of the preceding discussion may have seemed like a serial review of bits and pieces of scientific thinking, a discussion of hypotheses will bring these matters together.

The purpose of a hypothesis is to organize a study. If the hypothesis is carefully formed, all the steps of the scientific method follow, as does an outline for the project, a bibliography, a list of resources needed, and a specification of the measures appropriate to the study. The hypothesis provides the structure. A hypothesis is a sentence of a particularly well cultivated breed.

A hypothesis proposes a relationship between two or more variables. For example: *Political participation* IN-CREASES with *education.* This simple assertion can be seen as a hypothesis. It has a subject (the variable, *political participation*), a connective verb (a relationship, IN-CREASES), and an object (the variable, *education*).

To illustrate the point further:

> *Alienation* INCREASES with *poverty.*
> *Union members* are MORE LIKELY than nonunion members to *vote Democratic.*

Or, less obviously (and, for exercise, you can identify the variables and relations):

> Absence makes the heart grow fonder.
> An apple a day keeps the doctor away.
> Early to bed, early to rise makes men healthy, wealthy, and wise.

The importance of establishing a hypothesis correctly before starting off on a research task can hardly be over-estimated. First, the variables must be clearly specified and the relationship suggested between them must be stated precisely. Second, the variables must be measurable by some technique you are familiar with or competent to attempt. Third, the relationship specified has to be one that it is possible to demonstrate. If these rules are not followed, the hypothesis may be unwieldy, ridiculous, or maybe just too hard to research in view of the available resources.

So far, most of our examples of hypotheses have been quite simple. But to go from the straightforward to the bizarre, let me cite an experience in teaching scientific thinking. A student came to me with the following proposal for research.

> The fragile psycho-pathological type of double helical existence issuing from the precarious relationship of the colonizer and the colonized (which figuratively is similar to the relationship of Siamese twins) and their respective interaction within the colonial situation is psychologically effective, which ramifications lead to psychological maladjustments, i.e., neuroses which subsequently define the nature of the political particulars therein.

That was just the beginning of the proposal! In all that confusing language, there are lots of variables and many relationships. Sorting it out, however, yields two hypotheses. We cut it down to:

> *Colonialism is associated with neurotic behavior by colonizer and colonial.*

This neurotic behavior influences the political structure of colonialism.

These two hypotheses, large as they are, were somewhat manageable. The concept "colonialism" describes a well-established political situation. The connective "is associated with" was a retreat from saying "causes"—a precaution taken in view of the limited research resources available to the student. "Neurotic behavior" is a tricky concept, but it has parentage in the literature of psychoanalytic theory; there are behaviors that can respectably be labeled neurotic. From there it became a matter of showing the links between the kinds of neurotic, self-destructive behavior that occur in colonial situations to the repressive and authoritarian patterns of colonial politics.

Had the student accomplished all that these hypotheses imply by way of evidence-gathering, measurement, and evaluation, he would have been in line for a Ph.D. As long as he and I knew that he was just scratching the surface, his paper (bravely entitled "Colonialism: A Game for Neurotics") was good enough for undergraduate requirements.

One of the things this example illustrates is that there is often a prior step to hypothesis formation. The step is called *problem reformulation.* In the preceding example, we began with a generalized concern about colonialism and neurosis. The student elaborated that concern into a complex description of the problem. We narrowed it down by specifying variables and relationships into something that could be dealt with, at least in a general way.

One of the arts of social science is skillful problem reformulation. Reformulation requires, in addition to some analytic common sense, the ability to see the variables in a situation and the possible relationships between them. A good first step is to break the problem into its component variables and relationships. Writing down lists of the hypotheses associated with a problem enables you to select the ones that answer two questions: (1) Which hypotheses are crucial to the solution of the whole problem? and (2) For which hypotheses is there information within the range of your resources? Sometimes these questions force some unpleasant choices, but they help to prevent arriving at the end of a research effort with nothing substantial on which to hang a conclusion. The example above on "Colonialism and Neurosis" illustrates the point.

The Scientific Method

The technique known as the scientific method is quite commonsensical. The model inquiry proceeds by steps that include:

1. A *hypothesis* about the relation of one variable to another or to a situation.
2. A *reality-test* where the variables under examination are placed in a measurable relation to an outcome.
3. An *evaluation* in which the measured relationship is compared with the original hypothesis.
4. *Suggestions* about the significance of the findings, factors involved in the test that may have distorted the results, and other hypotheses that the inquiry brings to mind.

33

While we have sketched here the bare bones of the scientific method, the actual procedure of research does not always start directly with hypothesis formation. As a preliminary to stating hypotheses, social scientists will often examine the data collected in a subject area to see if there are connections between the variables in that area. The relationships brought to light by various statistical processes frequently suggest the hypotheses it would be fruitful to explore. Occasionally, simply getting involved with a set of data triggers an interesting thought, a chance insight, or a new idea. A great quantity of data has been generated over the past dozen years, so researchers can usually avoid having to begin at the beginning with every inquiry. The analysis of existing data can be extremely helpful in isolating new data needed to test a crucial relationship.

This is only an outline of the scientific method. In the hands of a skilled analyst, other elements are introduced, such as the use of alternative forms of measuring results, detailed conceptual analysis of the variable description, relationships between one's own study and others, tests of the validity of the measuring instruments, the use of experimental and control groups, and, equally important, careful conjecture that goes beyond what is established in the test itself. These embellishments on the methodology, however, relate more to the tools used in carrying on the method than the method itself.

The point is that *the scientific method seeks to test thoughts against reality in a disciplined manner, with each step in the process made explicit.*

Consider the differences between two kinds of studies: (1) An empirical scientific study in which the author states his or her values, forms hypotheses, lays out a testing procedure, carefully selects and discusses measurements, produces a specific result, and relates this to the hypotheses. (2) A nonscientific study in which the author expresses values, develops a general thesis, examines relevant examples, and states the conclusions.

Notice that the tension between thought and investigation is present in both studies. But one important difference is the feasibility of checking the validity of the conclusions in the first example as opposed to the second, by repeating the study. "Replication" is the word social scientists use to indicate the ability to reproduce a study as a way of checking on its validity. Replication constitutes a very strong test of a good study because it can reveal the errors that might have crept in through the procedures and evaluative judgments contained in the principal study.

A second difficulty with a nonscientific study lies in the problem of relating one study to another. Have you ever been annoyed in a discussion when someone asks you to "define your terms"? Have you ever gotten into arguments that begin with, "How can you tell that is true?" A good scientific study presents all the information needed to see what took place. If standard variable descriptions are used, a study of alienation and its relation to work, for example, can easily be added to a study of alienation and its relation to alcoholism, or crime, or whatever. Different studies of the same variables using different measures can be compared to see if measurement techniques create alternative results. The point, once again, is that science regulates and specifies the relationship between thought and investigation in such a way that others may know what exactly has been done.

Not all social science can be rigorous and precise,

but the complex social problems we face need all the well-informed study we can develop. The organization and evaluation of that knowledge is almost as important as gathering it in the first place. History is littered with the wreckage of poorly conceived social theories.

CONCEPTS INTRODUCED

Concept	Hypothesis
Variable	Scientific method
Discrete quantification	Reality-testing
Continuous quantification	Replication
Measurement	

OUTLINE

CHAPTER THREE

STRATEGIES

"At the most fundamental level, knowledge is organized experience and the search for knowledge is a search for patterns of organization. The organization is always created and not discovered."

EUGENE MEEHAN

Observant readers will notice that two words, usually thought to be integral to the scientific method, rarely appear in this book. They are "fact" and "truth." What both words have in common is an air of absolutism that misleads those who become involved in the scientific approach to learning. "Fact" means, according to its word root, "a thing done." That things do get done is not disputed, but the trouble is that "things done" are perceived not by some neutral omnipotent observer, but by people. People have limited powers of perception and structures of interest that influence how they see the world. Science is a process for controlling these perceptions by making them as explicit and open to examination as possible. But the results of scientific procedure must always be taken as just that, an *attempt* to control a process that our very humanity makes it difficult, if not impossible, totally to control.

For working purposes, social scientists generally regard a fact as "a particular ordering of reality in terms of a theoretical interest." [1] Such a statement means that anything identified as a fact must be seen to have tied to it the particular interests the observer brings to the study of the phenomenon. Further than that we cannot usefully go, for a philosophical forest looms in which subtle questions are raised about whether a tree that falls undetected by human perception has really fallen, since we can't know that it did.

The term "truth" is red meat for philosophers, and they are welcome to it. Science prefers to operate in the less lofty region of falsifiable statements that can be tested by evidence, and verifiable observations that can be checked by someone else. Every good scientific proposition or generalization is stated in such a way that sub-

---

[1] David Easton, *The Political System* (New York: Knopf, 1953), p. 53.

sequent observations may either provide supporting evidence or evidence that raises questions about the accuracy of the proposition. By making the degree of verification a permanent consideration in science, a good many rash conclusions can be avoided.

"What, then, are we to believe in?" might be the response to this noncommittal attitude toward fact and truth. If you want something absolute to believe in, it must be found outside of science. Science is a working procedure for answering questions by the refinement of experience. Scientists may develop theories of awe-inspiring power, but the way such theories meet our very human needs for belief is a personal matter separate from the meaning of science for inquiry. To "believe in science" means no more or less than to be committed to judgments based on reality-testing rather than on some other kind of evidence or mental process.

You are now familiar with basic elements of science, such as variables, measurements, and hypotheses. In this chapter we will concentrate on how to shape ideas about the world into a form that allows for reality-testing. Then the process of reality-testing will be broken down into its parts. Finally, we will see what evaluative steps need to be taken for understanding the results of research. The following remarks are designed as a step-by-step guide to scientific analysis. However, it must be realized that we are trying to capture only the most significant points of scientific procedure, not the finer points or the intricacies a sophisticated researcher would want to introduce. The following chapter, entitled "Refinements," adds to each element some ideas for increasing the power of your research strategy.

Please bear in mind that all we are doing here is

regulating what is natural to human thought: a tension between thought and reality-testing. So this chapter is organized into three sections: thinking the problem over, reality-testing, and understanding the results.

Thinking the Problem Over

The hardest problem in scientific thinking occurs at the very beginning. Once you have solved it, other steps fall into place. This is the problem of limiting the topic, or, more positively, isolating that approach to the topic that will most efficiently get at the thing you want to understand. Most students have had the experience of writing a long, rambling, poorly focused paper. As the need for conclusions looms with the final pages, there occasionally arises the awful feeling that from what has been said reasonably and with evidence, little that is useful can be firmly concluded. The reason for such an inglorious end can usually be found in the beginning.

Focus

Since most of us are not trained to think in terms of hypotheses, it is best to start writing things down in the way they occur to the mind: a sequence of ideas, thoughts, and notions. Ask yourself, Why am I interested in this? What is it that I am really after? See what happens. You may start with a broad topic: "Everyone seems so unhappy; people don't like their jobs; there's a general feeling of fatalism; modern society doesn't seem to have much place for the creative person." Big subjects, but there is a

theme here about the nature of modern working conditions and feelings of unhappiness.

At this stage it is a good idea to try to capture these
thoughts in a paragraph or two. Get it on paper! Some
general reading is a good idea. It helps to map out the
areas of investigation. Too much reading may be a bad
idea. Don't try to get into your actual research until you
have thought through the larger frame of the problem.

Suppose you wind up with two paragraphs like this:

> Society seems to be in an uproar. People are
> unhappy with their lives. Families are breaking
> down; violence is on the increase; people seem to
> feel that the world is cruel and headed for
> destruction. Karl Marx pointed out that people's
> social attitudes arise from their work lives. The
> main feature of contemporary work is the high
> degree of impersonalism.
>
> If people are making a living doing jobs that
> are not creative, they may feel powerless to control
> their own existence. It's a dangerous situation
> because these feelings could lead to extreme political
> behavior, such as violence, or total submission to
> leaders with crazy political ideas.

These paragraphs actually contain a number of variables, a network of relationships, and a whole series of
hypotheses. But at least there is some indication of the
possibilities for a more focused study.

At this point two levels of study could be mounted:
descriptive and *relational*. A *descriptive* study collects
facts about a situation. One might describe an institution,
event, or behavior, or some combination of these. Good
description is the beginning of a science. Leonardo da

Vinci's masterful notes and drawings of human anatomy enabled generations of medical scientists to advance their understanding of the body. Some specialized descriptive studies analyze information about a single variable, for example, the breakdown of families. What does it consist of? How much of it is going on? When does it occur most frequently? These studies are valuable sources for higher forms of analysis.

Relational analysis examines connections between things. The basic form consists of probing the links between one variable and another. The relation between education and voting, for example, or between intelligence and financial success. A series of relational studies can form the base for causal analysis, that special type of relational study in which the most powerful of connections between variables is isolated.

The initial thoughts on the topic given in the paragraphs above seem to imply a whole series of relations. If you are impatient to get to the root of the situation, a relational analysis of some aspect of the general problem of social uproar might be most satisfying.

Hypothesis Formation

With the topic narrowed somewhat, hypothesis formation becomes easier. The question is twofold: What are the essential variables? What are the relations between them? One intriguing piece of the problem sketched above involves two variables: *job* and *feelings of fatalism*. The paragraphs that were written suggest a link between the two. What is the nature of that link? What word expresses that relationship? If we leave aside causal analysis, the suggested relationship is a simple one: boring jobs are positively associated with feelings of fatalism. Or, more precisely: A job that is uncreative is more likely to be associated with feelings of fatalism than one that is creative.

Even with all these words, we still have only two variables and one relationship: *boring jobs* ASSOCIATED WITH *fatalism*. Most studies, of course, contain several hypotheses, possibly interconnected as elements of one larger thesis. But for purposes of illustration we will stay with something less demanding.

Operationalizing Variables

To operationalize a variable means putting the variable in a form that permits some kind of measurement. Translating a variable into something measurable is a tricky process. If it is done right, two conditions will be met: (1) the operational version fits the meaning of the original variable as closely as possible; (2) the measurement(s) indicated can be done accurately with available resources.

How does one operationalize a variable like *jobs?* The key is in the statement of the hypothesis. Under discussion here is a specific characteristic of jobs: the variation involves creativity—more of it versus less of it. The operationalization has to do with classifying jobs according to how creative they are. What are the characteristics of an uncreative job? Little control over the work, repetitiveness, minimal skill. This sounds like assembly-line work. If assembly-line work is uncreative, what is creative? A job that involves some individual control and application of skill. Maybe an artist has a creative job, or a teacher, or someone who manipulates technological processes.

Here enters another consideration. It would be easier if the research could be confined to one location. A factory often includes a variety of jobs. Are there any creative jobs in a factory? Some persons do skilled work that requires judgment. Others maintain and repair the machinery that moves the assembly line. Least creative are the basically repetitive assembly jobs.

What emerges here is an operationalization of the variable *jobs* in terms of three categories: line, repair, and skilled. These categories cover some significant part of the dimension of creativity in jobs.

The next task is to operationalize feelings of fatalism. The most obvious way to get at feelings is to ask about them. You might question a sample of workers in each category, "Do you feel fatalistic?" The term "fatalism" itself has some problems, however. It is a big word. Also, it isn't a word that workers commonly use. A less obvious way of operationalizing this variable, and one that might get you closer to everyday concerns, would be to ask some questions about common attitudes that reveal fatalistic feelings.

At this point, we will begin to observe the strategy actually used in a study by Lewis Lipsitz, entitled "Work Life and Political Attitudes: A Study of Manual Workers." [2] The article is reprinted, for convenience of reference, as an appendix to this book. The Lipsitz study is an example of a well-constructed and carefully presented research project. The format he uses in discussing the theoretical context of the study, the steps taken in testing

[2] In *The American Political Science Review* 58 (December 1964): 951–962.

hypotheses, and the larger meaning of his results provide a model of the form appropriate to research reporting.

In operationalizing the variable *fatalism*, Lipsitz put four questions to his sample of workers:

1. Will men and nations always fight wars with one another?
2. Will there always be poverty in the world?
3. Do you think the ordinary man is helpless to change some aspect of government he doesn't like, or is there something he can do about it?
4. Some people say they can plan ahead for long-range goals and then carry out their plans. Others say, "Whatever's going to be is going to be and there's no sense planning." How do you feel about it? [3]

The handy thing about these questions is that responses can be easily divided into positive and negative. Someone who answers that "war and poverty are inevitable," "people are helpless to change politics," and "there isn't any use in planning ahead" could be considered fatalistic. Three of four negative responses would be evidence of more fatalism than one of four negative responses.

What we have here is a four-item scale that gives us the possibility of scoring responses in terms of the level of fatalism. There could be a score of zero, one, two, three, or four fatalistic responses.

Both variables, *jobs* and *fatalism*, have now been

[3] Appendix. p. 136. We do not discuss the construction of scales in this text. For a detailed treatment of scales, see Hubert Blalock and Ann Blalock, *Methodology in Social Research* (New York: McGraw-Hill, 1968), Chapter 3, "Attitude Measurement," by Harry Upshaw, pp. 60–108.

operationalized. Both can be measured in terms of their internal variation. Jobs are classified by their level of creativity, and fatalism is measured by a four-item scale. With the variables operationalized, the stage is set for organizing the whole inquiry.

Reality-Testing

Organizing the Bibliography

With a hypothesis in mind, it is a good idea now to do some additional reading before actually beginning research. This will help you to check your formulation of hypotheses and operationalization of variables against other efforts. Articles, books, and journal reports are all valuable sources for information and background. Often a single journal article on the same general topic will contain footnotes and bibliography that can guide you to most of the significant literature on the subject. A more sophisticated researcher would take this step first—it can save a lot of time in the thinking-it-over stage. However, beginning students often come to problems of social analysis "fresh."

Doing Research

Not many students could mount the kind of research effort suggested here. However, for instructional purposes, it is sufficient to see how an example of social science research works so that your own project can be formulated with the clearest possible strategy.

Lipsitz secured the cooperation of managers and union leaders in an auto factory in New Jersey. The hypothesis under discussion was one of a number of propositions being tested on the general subject of work life and political attitudes.

Collecting the data involves essentially two operations. The jobs first have to be classified in terms of the operational categories set up for the variable. As it happens, the distinctions of line, repair, and skilled fit nicely with the descriptions used in the plant.

A representative sample of workers must then be drawn unless there are sufficient resources to do the whole population. Although we will not discuss here what is involved in obtaining a representative sample, a description of that process can be found in Chapter Four.

Each respondent must be categorized by job. Second, each worker must be asked to answer the questions in the fatalism scale. The nature of the questions permits an oral or written response and the interviewer does the classifying of answers into positive and negative. The way the questions are asked is important. If the questions were asked by someone identified with the management, a worker might be suspicious that he was being personally evaluated in some way. If the questions were asked by an interviewer who seemed to encourage a certain kind of answer by his or her manner or appearance, the results would not be accurate. The interview process must be made as neutral and low-profile as possible.

Tallying the results is a simple process. Record the numbers of those with zero, one, two, three, four fatalistic responses by each category of worker. In the Lipsitz study, the answers were recorded for workers in each job category (Table 3.1).[4]

---

[4] Appendix, p. 136.

TABLE 3.1

Number of Fatalistic Answers

Job	None	One	Two	Three	Four
Line	0	2	3	5	2
Repair	3	2	5	2	2
Skilled	3	6	3	3	0

Looking at the data in this bare form, it is hard to see what the relationship is between the two variables, *jobs* and *fatalism*. How can these data be summarized in a way that will permit some general conclusion? Lipsitz employed an elementary device. He calculated the average number of fatalistic responses for each category of worker.

The higher the average (i.e., the more positive responses to the fatalism question), the more fatalistic the category of worker. The results are shown in Table 3.2.[5]

TABLE 3.2

Job	Average Fatalism Score	
Line	2.58	$(0 \times 0)+(2 \times 1)+(3 \times 2)+(5 \times 3)+(4 \times 2) = 31\frac{1}{12}$ responses
Repair	1.86	
Skilled	1.40	

The average score permits some generalization about the hypothesis: *boring jobs are positively associated with feelings of fatalism.* The study does demonstrate a positive association: the more boring the job, the higher the fatalism score. This may seem to have provided a happy

[5] Appendix, p. 136.

ending to the study, but there is more to concluding a research effort than simply saying, "See, I was right (or wrong)!"

Analyzing the Results

Results need to be placed in perspective. In this study, the difference in the average fatalism score varies by 1.18 points, from 1.40 for skilled workers to 2.58 for line workers. That variation is large enough to be worth comment, but a variation of, for example, .50 would be a pretty slim number to hang a hypothesis on. Considering the largest possible variation of 5.00 (from zero for the skilled category to 5.00 for the line category), we can also see that the association is not absolute by any means. The first step in analyzing the results, then, is to see how they fit in terms of the range of possible variation.

A second step is to compare the results with other studies along the same lines. Do the results regarding fatalism fit in with other efforts to relate boring jobs to similar attitudes such as powerlessness, distrust, and feelings of personal ineffectiveness? By consulting other reality-tests, you can gain perspective on the utility of the one you have constructed. At the same time, other studies can provide a general check on your findings.

Understanding the Results

Evaluating Variable Operationalization

Now that you have some research experience with the subject, rethink each step of the strategy in light of what

51

happened. There is a big difference between thinking of a way to operationalize a variable and having it work as expected in the process of research.

A list of questions for this project would be:

1. Did the job categories work out, or were there jobs that were hard to define as line, repair, or skilled? Were there differences within categories such as some line jobs that were less boring than others? Did some skilled jobs resemble line jobs?

2. Are you sure workers properly identified which kind of job they held? Maybe someone thought of himself as a skilled line worker and so indicated that he held a skilled job. (A famous example of the error involved in self-identification of operational categories can be found in polls where the respondent is asked to indicate whether he or she is lower, middle, or upper class. Because the respondent's interpretation might differ from the definitions an interviewer would want to use, the answers are often misleading.)

3. Did the interview questions seem to get at the dimension of fatalism? If you encourage open-ended responses in a questionnaire, as well as forced-choice items, it is possible to get a feel for the way the questions have been interpreted. Someone might answer, "Yes, war and poverty are inevitable and average people can't plan their lives or influence politics, but this is the greatest nation in the world, God is obviously on our side, and the future belongs to us. So there!" No fatalist, this individual.

There is also the problem of a person's state of mind in answering a question. Any number of factors could influence responses. Liquor can't be sold in many states on election day so as to avoid obscuring the public vision. Beyond chemical disturbance is the possibility of other intervening events—if recent rumors of a lay-off threaten line workers (though not others), they may be excused for feeling particularly fatalistic at the time. A good deal of social science research ignores the time dimension. The answer, obviously, is to repeat studies in different times and places. If you ask college students to fill out questionnaires, be ready for the campus wit. The jokers, the devious, and the perverse can foul up a questionnaire in many ways.

Another possible form of interference with honest responses arises from respondents who feel there is something fishy about the project, the researcher, the questions, or the presumed confidentiality of the responses. An erstwhile sophomore coed recently polled the faculty of a church college in which a friend of mine teaches about their personal use of marijuana. She did these interviews in person and assured the faculty that each response would be "confidential"—the data summaries were to be broken down by department and rank, and the final paper would then be placed in the library. However, a "liberated" junior faculty member in a small department might conceivably be wary of the promised confidentiality and be less than honest in responding to such an invitation to persecution if not prosecution.

In dealing with people, science does not substitute for savvy.

Were the Measures Any Good?

Self-criticism isn't a particularly welcome task, but in social science it serves two specific purposes. Obviously, it helps to reexamine a project after you've finished to be sure that the steps along the way are sufficiently well done to lead directly to the conclusion. Reexamination serves another function, however. In dealing with something as slippery as the measurement of social phenomena, whatever is learned in the development and use of measures needs to be shared. A measure can look very impressive at the outset of an inquiry. The experience gained in actually using it, however, may turn up some unexpected weaknesses that, if stated as part of the results, can save someone else a lot of work.

In the scale used in the example, the questions do measure a kind of fatalism. But the questions all deal with large issues framed in generalities: the inevitability of war, the omnipresence of poverty, the possibility of individuals influencing government, and the ability of people to plan ahead. A question might be raised about whether these are the indicators of fatalism closest to people's daily lives. Concerns about war, poverty, politics, and planning are significant, but maybe not as pressing as worries about job security, family well-being, and physical threats, not to mention the noise in the car engine, the plan for the weekend, and the overdraft notice from the bank. The questions Lipsitz used for measuring fatalism could be criticized for not being close enough to the most relevant personal issues.[6]

Does this criticism invalidate the measure? No. It simply tells you more clearly what may or may not have been measured. A little more research in the field might turn up other measurements of fatalism using scales that

---

[6] In the article, Lipsitz uses a variety of measures to get at different aspects of the political consequences of factory work.

approach personal issues more directly. A comparison of findings would increase the usefulness of your results.

Another possible criticism involves the statistics used to summarize the measures. Remember that Lipsitz used the average of scores for each job category. It would be worth checking to see what the pattern of responses is *within* each job category. Table 3.3 repeats the "raw" data given in Table 3.1.

TABLE 3.3

Number of Fatalistic Answers

Job	None	One	Two	Three	Four	Average
Line	0	2	3	5	2	2.58
Repair	3	2	5	2	2	1.86
Skilled	3	6	3	3	0	1.40

While the average tells something about the characteristics of people in each job category, it also conceals important information. Considered in terms of individual workers, it turns out that there is quite a wide variety of responses in each category. Three skilled workers gave three fatalistic answers, which makes them more fatalistic than five of the line workers and ten of the repair workers (those who gave less than three fatalistic answers).[7] Again, this doesn't make the results meaningless, it just qualifies them. It would be wrong to say that you can

---

[7] Lipsitz examined his results more carefully than I have reported here. He looked at which questions received the most frequent positive responses, for example, and found interesting differences among job categories in their fatalism about war as opposed to poverty and other issues. Appendix, pp. 137–140.

predict *with certainty* that an individual line worker is more fatalistic than an individual skilled worker. The average scores suggest that the odds are slightly in favor of such a prediction being correct, but it's nothing to bet the rent on.

Assorted mystics through the ages have made much of examining the entrails of birds for portents and predictions of the future. Those skilled in statistical criticism are probably the modern heirs of this profession, particularly in their ability to find good news and bad news in any given statistic. That statistics do not provide, in and of themselves, precise answers to social inquiries, surprises some and comforts others. It is easy to say that statistics can lie, or that they never quite get the whole message across, and are therefore useless. There is a nasty old joke that indirectly suggests the right perspective on statistics: "How's your wife?" For which the punch line is, "Compared to what?" Compared to language concepts such as "more," "less," "a whole bunch," or "a little bit," statistics can be more precise.

The wrong statistic can be used as easily as the wrong word, and to be scientific is no substitute for common sense. As you learn more about statistics, you will find that researchers typically use several statistics to summarize a situation, rather than relying on a single indicator, such as an average, in order to compensate for the faults of any particular statistic.

How Do Your Findings Fit with Theories in the Field?

Although we have said very little about the role of theory in research up to now, theory is exceedingly important in the development of social science. However, theory doesn't become important until you have gotten further down the road of social scientific inquiry. Most beginning researchers are motivated more by a particular question or puzzle than by the effort to prove or disprove some large-size explanation of the world. In any event, dealing in big-time theory requires considerable experience and effort.

Volumes have been written about what theory is and isn't. For our purposes, theory is a set of related propositions that suggests why events occur in the manner that they do. Theory abounds in the most ordinary transactions of life: there are theories of everything from the pay-off of pinball machines to the inner meaning of Peanuts cartoons. The point of any science is to develop a set of theories to explain the events within their range of observation.

While a simple experiment or inquiry may answer some puzzle that is on your mind, it may also relate in interesting ways to more general issues that are contained within theories of the subject. It is mildly interesting to know that certain kinds of jobs increase the tendency toward personal fatalism—but it is a lot more interesting if that finding can be fitted in with a whole set of ideas about the human condition as it relates to work, or to the general problem (with which we started) of the breakdown of industrialized society. These are large theoretical perspectives, but theory doesn't have to be grand to be good. There are less global theories that explain key pieces of events.

Lipsitz, in the example we cite, begins and ends his article with a wide-ranging discussion of theory and research on the relationship between industrialization and democracy. He cites a number of other scholars who have probed the question of the connection between the kinds of work industrialization creates, the political attitudes associated with factory work, and the way such attitudes do or do not fit in with the requirements of democratic society.

Similarly, in the exercise of writing down a couple of paragraphs on the general topic earlier in this chapter, theory surfaced in the mention of Marx and in the generalized concern with the state of modern society. If, as the Lipsitz study suggests, jobs at the bottom of the industrial order are associated with feelings of political and personal fatalism, this says something about the viability of a political system that depends on at least minimal levels of political concern and activism. An economic system that consigns large numbers of people to boring, repetitive jobs may undermine the conditions for participation in democratic government by causing widespread apathy and alienation.

In writing up the results of a study, refer back to the general readings you have done. Also, if time allows, do some more investigation of what other people have found out about jobs, boredom, and the future of society.

A noteworthy scientist once commented that "science is observation," by which he meant to suggest that getting all wound up in the details of experimental and control groups, statistics, and the rest can obscure the purpose of scientific inquiry: using your head to understand what is going on.[8] There is no such thing as the perfect experi-

---

[8] Robert Hodes, "Aims and Methods of Scientific Research," Occasional Paper No. 9 (New York: American Institute of Marxist Studies, 1968), pp. 11–14.

ment that explains everything about a given phenomenon. Where science as method ends, scientists as *people* take over. Scientific procedure is lifeless by itself. In the hands of an imaginative researcher it becomes a very useful tool, but the mind is a far more subtle instrument than any set of procedures for investigation.

In relating your work to theory and in speculating about its larger consequences, you have a chance to be imaginative and creative, though not undisciplined or completely fanciful. Fourier, a French socialist, extended the observation that people work better and are happier in communes to the notion that advances in human understanding would cause world history to ascend (through hundreds of years) to a situation so utopian that every day would begin with a parade, the oceans would turn into lemonade, and we would be transported across the seas by friendly whales. That's a bit much.

CONCEPTS INTRODUCED

Fact
Truth
Falsifiable statements
Verifiable observations
Descriptive study

Relational analysis
Variable operationalization
Research bibliography
Theory

OUTLINE

CHAPTER FOUR

REFINEMENTS

"Enthusiasm and deep conviction are necessary if men are to explore all the possibilities of any new idea, and later experience can be relied on either to confirm or to moderate the initial claims—for science flourishes on a double programme of speculative liberty and unsparing criticism."

STEPHEN TOULMIN and
JUNE GOODFIELD

Developing a sense for the methodology of social science resembles learning to play pool. The basic elements of each are simple: in pool, a table, some balls, and a stick; in social science, variables, measurements, and hypotheses. Up to now, we have been looking at the simple shots: a

hypothesis with two fairly obvious variables and a measurement of the relations between them. In science, as
in pool, the more elaborate strategies are variations on
the basic technique. A good pool player never tries a
harder shot than absolutely necessary; so also with a social
scientist. Likewise, professionals in both fields have had
to invent techniques for minimizing error and getting
around obstacles. In this chapter we will discuss the elements in a slightly different order from previous chapters
—hypotheses, variables, and measurements—and explore
some refinements of each. Or, in other words, we'll illustrate some bank shots in the corner pocket.

Hypotheses

Hypotheses do not spring full-blown from the intellect
unencumbered by a web of thoughts and preferences.
Like any other artifact of human behavior, a hypothesis is
part of a mosaic of intentions, learnings, and concerns.
Social scientists have debated long and hard over how
to deal with this reality. Some have preferred that the
researcher do everything possible to forget values and
other biases in order to concentrate on "objectively" pursuing work in the name of professional social science.
Others have insisted that ignoring the origins of a hypothesis is inefficient because it leads the researcher to
ignore basic factors in his or her own approach to data.
And, just as hypotheses do not emerge from a value
vacuum, neither are the results of research presented to
a neutral environment.

The debate over the role of values in research is
carried on in the shadow of the moral controversy over

those scientists who did the original research for atomic weapons in the 1940s. Their argument was that they were pursuing the path of science—the *uses* of science being the province of others. While social scientists have no atomic bombs to show for their efforts, the technology of social control that social science has begun to generate may well come to have power of a magnitude worthy of the same moral concern.

Aside from the moral issues about the uses of science, there is another whole set of questions related to how hypotheses fit with structures of thought such as theories, models or, to use a more recent word, paradigms. The formation of generalizable theory is, after all, the end object of the exercise. Thus the relations between theory and research require exploration.

Finally, there is the somewhat more mundane, operational matter of the kinds of relationships that can be built into hypotheses. These three topics—the roles of values, theories, and relationships in the formation of hypotheses—will be dealt with successively.

Values and Hypothesis Formation

The notion of values is in itself peculiar. Writers have often tried to come to grips with what a value is and how one value can be separated from another. The sticky part is that values are hard to isolate. I may believe in freedom, but not freedom to the exclusion of equality, or freedom for certain kinds of behavior, such as theft. Values occur in webs of mutually modifying conditions. The confused self we all experience often may be seen acting out different sets of values at different moments, with a larger pattern visible only over a substantial time period. Still there remains a kind of consistency to human character—enough so that we can and do make general estimates of the orientation to life that people have.

Social scientists generally have resolved the problem of the relation of values to research by recommending that one's value orientations be discussed in presenting a report of a project. Because values enter in so intimately in every step of forming a hypothesis, selecting measures, and evaluating conclusions, that is a fair request. However, the specification cannot be an afterthought. The role of values has to be squarely faced at the outset of inquiry. Unless that is done, you may not see what your values are doing to your research. For example, someone who is strongly religious might do research on dating habits involving questions that are premised on the immorality of premarital intercourse. The questions used might easily reflect such a bias and invite respondents to condemn a practice that they approve.

Of Theories, Models, and Paradigms

The relationship of a hypothesis, or an inquiry, to theories and models of phenomena seems common-sensical but becomes steadily more complicated when authors try to set down the relationship in writing. We know what a theory is—a set of related propositions that attempts to explain, and sometimes to predict, a set of events. By now we also know what a hypothesis is. In a rough sense, a theory is a collection of hypotheses linked together by some kind of logical framework. The term "theory" connotes a degree of uncertainty about whether the understanding it offers is valid and correct. Theories, then, are tentative formulations. That which has been demonstrated to defy falsification usually is embodied in sets of "laws" and axioms.

Two other terms enter into the discussion. Scientists use the term "model" to convey an implication of greater order and system in a theory. Economists, for instance, are heavily involved in efforts to create theoretical models of the economy in which all the major variables associated with economic performance are related mathematically. On the other hand, the term "paradigm," which comes from a Latin root meaning "pattern," refers to a larger frame of understanding, shared by a wider community of scientists, that organizes smaller-scale theories and inquiries. For generations in antiquity, astronomy was dominated by a paradigm that placed earth at the center of the universe. Early observers of the heavens tried to explain all other stellar phenomena within that context; ultimately, of course, the paradigm collapsed with the advent of a much more powerful explanation.

There are few laws and axioms in social science, some vague paradigms, a good many theories, and lately some intriguing models. For those at the outset of social scientific investigation, theory is best conceived of as a guide to inquiry—a way of organizing and economizing insight so as to avoid the trivial and isolate the significant.

Before talking in more operational terms about the relation of theory to hypotheses, one matter of perspective needs development. Just as language arises out of the experience of coming to grips with human needs, so also does theory arise from tasks the species faces.

The grandest theories of all are religious and philosophical, embracing huge orders of questions about the origin of the physical universe, the history of the species, the purposes of life, and the norms of behavior that are

"Dynamite, Mr. Gerston! You're the first person I ever heard use 'paradigm' in real life."

Drawing by Lorenz; © 1974 The New Yorker Magazine, Inc.

appropriate to a condition of virtue and, possibly, happiness. To the faithful, such theories are made true by belief in supernatural phenomena. These kinds of theories appear to exist embedded in the larger cosmos of our existence awaiting our arrival at understanding.

Social science, by contrast, generally operates from a different perspective on theory. The most conventional posture for a social scientist is one of pragmatism: a theory is only as good as its present and potential uses in the service of human needs. It is tempting, but misleading, to conceive of theory as something rocklike and immobile behind the whizz and blur of daily experience.

Rather, theory is a sometimes ingenious creation of human beings in their quest for need fulfillment. People create theories in proportion to needs, and the theories they create can be either functional or disfunctional to those needs.

From this point of view, a theory could contain a complete system of categories and the relationships between them but still be useless. If, for example, one were to categorize the world in terms of tall things and short things and characterize all the relationships between them, a theory would have been born, but it would be one of dubious utility—not false, but useless.

With that perspective in mind, there are two general modes by which theory comes into play in social science: inductive and deductive. Induction refers to building theory through the accumulation and summation of a variety of inquiries. Deduction has to do with using the logic of a theory to generate propositions that can then be tested.

The most popular image of science has researchers collecting bits of information through a gradual process of investigation and forming them into theories. The test then becomes whether or not the theory explains what is known about a phenomenon. The danger in accepting the simple view of science as induction is that the inquiries that form the theory's base may have been undertaken from a value perspective or a commitment to fundamental categories that prejudges the phenomenon—leading in due course to a theory that validates the original biases. Scientific procedure is designed to make this difficult because of the requirement that the propositions in a theory must be put in falsifiable form, that is, they must be subject to testing. As clear as that requirement would seem to be, social investigation is so value-laden and the tools for reality-testing so limited that mistaken judgments can easily be made.

Deduction is the less acknowledged form for relating theory to research. However, under pressure of attack from critics of the supposedly "objective" nature of social science, researchers are beginning to understand that deduction enters subtly into the formation of basic concepts commonly used in hypotheses. In American culture, the pervasive conditioning and reinforced commitment to a capitalist political-economic system has caused many political scientists, sociologists, and economists to take our system as the norm of the good society and to cast all nonmarket patterns of behavior into such pejorative categories as deviant, counterproductive, apathetic, and so on. The connotations of these labels are, in a real sense, deduced from a larger theory that implies the naturalness or rightness of one system of political economy.

Proceeding from such culturebound assumptions, it becomes easier to argue that behavior that is against an individual's material self-interest is in fact irrational and requires treatment or even forcible correction. In fact, the behavior under consideration may be serving needs repressed in a capitalist society and therefore be functional in adapting to a difficult environment, for instance, the behavior of the poor person who buys a fancy car. Owning a car may be the one opportunity for the person to be alone, to give the appearance of success, to regard himself or herself as someone of consequence, and to attract attention from an otherwise uncaring world. That the payments decimate the food budget may strike the middle-class observer as foolish largely because middle-class observers, those with jobs at any rate, do not suffer

the stress of constant rejection and personal immisera-
tion.

Since deduction is a natural pattern of thought, it
needs to be harnessed to scientific exploration. Very often
deductions from theory provide the basic agenda of a field
of inquiry. Established theories are guides to the solution
of many particular puzzles. The deductive "route" is well
worth trying before starting anew in the task of explanation.

There is no need to carry this navel-gazing about induction and deduction too far. A good scientific inquiry
always contains those elements that make it possible for
others who have differing perspectives to judge its worth.
The principal reason to keep these points in mind is to be
conscious of self-delusion and of the ways others are misleading in their presentation of scientific findings.

Long before you are able to deal with the formation
of theories, you will be a consumer of theory retailed by
others. In utilizing research results, there is a precaution-
ary question that needs to be asked about the theory in
terms of which the results are conceived to be meaningful.
It is similar to the question about the values behind an inquiry, and it consists of understanding the theoretical perspective from which an inquiry is undertaken. Never read
a social science work without paying careful attention to
the introduction and preface—therein usually lies the key
as to what the author's commitments are.

At the same time, do not be afraid to play with theoretical explanation as a guide to your own efforts. Science
is very democratic and anyone can take an investigative
potshot at a theory or try to extend it in new ways. By
becoming aware of the predominant theories in a field,

you can save some of your own time by borrowing their vision to see what the possible explanations of a phenomenon are.

Relationships in Hypotheses

Independent and Dependent Variables   Not all variables are equal. If social science managed only to show that prejudice is associated with ignorance, youth with rebellion, and IQ with breast-feeding, they wouldn't have done as much as the culture has a right to expect. Are people prejudiced because they are ignorant, or ignorant because they wear the blinders of prejudice? Which precedes the other? I almost said, which *causes* the other, but did not since demonstrating causation, as we will see shortly, requires very elaborate procedures. The notion of independence and dependence in variables is a way of sneaking up on the question of causation without trying to go the whole distance.

An *independent* variable is one that influences another variable, called the *dependent* variable. As heat increases, air can hold more water. Heat is an independent variable, the amount of water suspended in the air, a dependent variable. If heat goes up, the air can hold more water. If the air is soggy and heat goes down, water starts falling out of the air—which even social scientists refer to as rain.

In the example presented in Chapter Three on boring jobs and feelings of fatalism, Lipsitz suggests that boring jobs are the independent variable and fatalism, the dependent variable. The creative possibilities of a job influence the kinds of attitudes people have about life in general. However, it might work the other way around—

fatalistic attitudes could lead people to take jobs that involve little creativity.

There's nothing very tricky about the notion of independence and dependence. But there is something tricky about the fact that the relationship of independence and dependence is a figment of the researcher's imagination until demonstrated convincingly. Researchers *hypothesize* relationships of independence and dependence: they imagine them, they invent them, and then they try by reality-testing to see if the relationships actually work out that way.

The question of independent and dependent variables can be more clearly understood when seen in the form social scientists are fondest of—tables. Tables are a method of presenting data, but behind a table is often a hypothesis that escapes the attention of the novice.

Consider Table 4.1. Which is the independent vari-

TABLE 4.1   POLITICAL ACTIVITY AMONG BLACKS
AND WHITES

	Blacks	*Whites*
Written or spoken to Congressman	13%	18%
Worked to elect a political candidate	12	11
Given money to a candidate or political party	11	17
Belong to a political club	10	12

NOTE: From William Brink and Louis Harris, *Black and White* (New York: Simon and Schuster, 1966). Data taken from a survey commissioned by *Newsweek* magazine in 1966, based on a national sample. N = 1,059 blacks and 1,088 whites.

able? Which the dependent variable? How would you reconstruct the hypothesis that this data supports?

The two variables are *race* and *political activity*.

71

What does the data say about the relationship between these two variables? The answer is that whites are slightly more involved than blacks in political activities. Race influences participation. Therefore, race is the presumed *independent* variable and participation is the *dependent* variable. To check on the assignment of the labels "independent" and "dependent," reverse the hypothesis: Could the level of political activity influence what race a person is? No.

Table 4.1 illustrates the form in which tables are usually presented. The independent variable is listed across the *top* and the dependent variable down the *side*. By presenting tables in this standard fashion, researchers can locate the relationship without having to think about it. Nevertheless, it is a very good practice when looking at a table to formulate the hypotheses it is supposed to test. The author may have reversed the usual location of the independent and dependent variables for reasons of emphasis, style, or simply convenience.

In the race-political activity illustration, the independent and dependent variables are easily identified. The relationship is nonreversible. That is not always the case. In one part of the Lipsitz study, he reports data on the mental health scores of male factory workers in their forties (Table 4.2).[1]

The relationship between the variables *job classification* and *mental health scores* in Table 4.2 could conceivably be stated either way, and Lipsitz recognizes this. It might be claimed that the level of occupation influences

[1] See Lipsitz, Appendix, p. 145.

TABLE 4.2

Job	Percentage with Good Mental Health Scores	Number in Category
Skilled	56%	45
High semiskilled	41	98
Ordinary semiskilled	38	82
Repetitive semiskilled	26	73
Repetitive machine-paced only (subdivision of preceding category)	16	32

mental health. A more creative job helps the mind to function better. The reverse is also possible: an individual's mental health may influence what kind of work he or she is able to get. Mentally distressed persons have a hard time getting skilled jobs. Lipsitz was interested in the first of these propositions and uses other evidence to establish that it is the more likely explanation of the two.[2] He was trying to suggest through measurements of several variables that assembly-line work may create attitudes that are not healthy in a democracy.

Notice in the example above that Lipsitz violates the rule of thumb about the placement of variables: his presumed independent variable, *job classification,* is located on the side and the dependent variable, *mental health scores*, is listed on the top of the table. The reasons for this are simply convenience: it saves space to do it that way. This is one more reason to formulate in your mind the hypothesis that is being tested in the tabular presentation of data.

[2] Appendix, note 20, p. 146.

Alternative, Antecedent, and Intervening Variables
One of the central problems in developing strong hypotheses lies in understanding how variables stand in relation to each other. In hypothesizing relationships between variables, you need to be aware of variables other than the ones you have selected that may be involved in producing changes in a relationship. Social scientists commonly refer to alternative, antecedent, and intervening variables.

All three terms have commonsense meanings. An alternative variable is an additional independent variable that influences changes in the dependent variable. An antecedent is something that comes before. The antecedent of birth is conception. To intervene means to come between. Richard M. Nixon was on his way to becoming the presidential master of ceremonies of the nation's Bicentennial when a custodian at the Watergate intervened by calling the police. We will illustrate each of these concepts more precisely.

If one considers the variables which influence whether a person votes, several appear: attitudes toward the system, the difficulty of registration procedures, the weather on election day, the person's level of information about politics, and so on. These are alternative variables. To establish the link between any one of these variables and voting participation is useful nonetheless, though a complete account of why people do or do not vote would have to include the influence of all the significant alternative variables.

A classic illustration of an antecedent variable comes from the history of research on voting behavior. It became obvious early on that more highly educated people tend to vote Republican. From that relationship, it could be implied that smart people are conservative. However, it turns out that there is a powerful antecedent variable which influences both the *level of education* and *voting behavior: parental wealth.* Those who are highly educated tend to come from wealthier families, and wealthier families are more likely to vote Republican. What was being measured in the correlation of *education* with *voting behavior* was really the influence of *parental wealth* on the political preferences of their children.

As for intervening variables, suppose you are told that Hollygood Bread has fewer calories per slice than six other brands. The advertising leads you to assume that the independent variable is Hollygood's special formula for low-calorie dough. You come to find out that the real reason for the difference is that the Hollygood Company slices its bread thinner than the others. The dough actually has about as many calories as Sunshaft Bread or even Wondergoo. The thinness of the slice is the intervening variable between quality of dough and calories per slice.

The way to avoid getting trapped by alternative, antecedent, and intervening variables is to do some thinking before formulating a hypothesis. Take the dependent variable and ask yourself what all the possible independent variables might be. If you want to explain why people are fatalistic, think of all the variables that could influence such a state of mind. There are other possibilities besides the nature of their work, such as money troubles, unrequited love, background characteristics, the weather, peer-group influences. You may decide to test the original independent variable anyway just to see how much association there is. In fact, most social phenomena, perhaps *all* social phenomena, are influenced by several variables. The point of worrying about alternative, antecedent, and intervening variables is not so much to discourage investigation of what interests you as to put it into perspective so that you do not confuse association with causation, of which more is said below.

Once you recognize the variables that have a significant influence on a dependent variable, there are ways of separating out the influence of one variable from another. The simplest technique is to "control" for one variable by holding it constant, while two others are tested for their relationship to each other. In the example of the connections between parental wealth, education, and voting behavior, one could select a sample of respondents with various levels of education from families of different wealth characteristics. If it turns out that highly educated children of wealthy families are predominantly Republican, and that highly educated children of poorer families are predominantly Democrat, you know that education is far less powerful than family wealth in shaping voting behavior. As your methodological experience and sophistication increase, you will discover a host of techniques by which these connections can be sorted out. The first step in approaching the problem of sorting out variables is to understand the different levels of relationships that are built into hypotheses.

Levels of Relationships in Hypotheses   The most distinctive characteristic of a hypothesis as opposed to most ordinary sentences is the care with which each term is specified. We have seen that selection of variables is a serious task in itself. So also with the relationships that are specified between variables. In order to stretch your imagination a little, it is worth considering systematically the possible relationships that can be expressed between two or more variables. They comprise a spectrum, and we will discuss briefly each of the relationships presented in Table 4.3.

TABLE 4.3

Relationship	Meaning
Null	No relationship is presumed to exist.
Inferential/ Correlative	A relationship is presumed, but it is a relationship that deals with degrees of influence of one variable on another.
Direct/Inverse	A specific correlative relationship is presumed in which one variable has a predictable association with another—either one variable increases as the other increases (direct) or one increases while the other decreases (inverse).
Causal	Changes in one variable are presumed to result from variations in another.

The null hypothesis is a rather ingenious creation. Remembering always that hypotheses are imagined relationships that are then put to the test, there is something to say for positing NO relationship and then testing to see if the null hypothesis can be DISproven, that is, it can be demonstrated that some relationship does indeed exist.

The utility of the null hypothesis is that the case is not prejudged—you are not caught defending a relationship specified beforehand. In addition to withholding commitment to a specific relationship, you are also leaving open the possibility that one of the more substantial relationships may characterize the connection between the variables. It may be that there is an inferential or correlative relationship that will emerge from the reality-test. There may even be a direct or inverse relationship, but those possibilities are left to emerge from the test itself.

The null hypothesis is admirably suited to a conservative strategy of social investigation. Causation requires an enormous burden of proof and is at the opposite end of the relationship spectrum from the null hypothesis. Disproving a null hypothesis requires only a demonstration that some connection does indeed appear when a hypothesis is put to the test.

Inferential and correlative relationships can be tested as a preliminary to moving in on causative relationships. The lesser relationships, while they are interesting in themselves, are also screening devices. If, in the example of the relation of alienation to menial work, a correlation that is statistically significant can be demonstrated, then there is some reason to press ahead with the work of separating out extraneous sources of error that may be responsible for the correlation. That done, the alternative sources of causation may be tested to see if a causal hypothesis might be justified.

Several things need to be understood about the relationship of causation. First, it is probably the end object of social science to decide what causes what. Therefore, there is tremendous interest in establishing causality. Second, it is the most difficult relationship to deal with because it demands the highest burden of proof. To prove that "A" CAUSES "B," you need to demonstrate that:

1. *A happens before B.* Obvious, isn't it?

2. *The occurrence of A is connected with the occurrence of B.* Obvious as well, but the connections of events are not always simple to discover. Some historians, for example, find a consistent link between the diets of reformers in the middle ages and the elaborateness of their

visions. Joan of Arc, it is claimed, ate the wrong things, fouled up her digestive system, and so became a visionary and temporary heroine!

3. *A causes B; there isn't some other variable (C) that eliminates the variation in B associated with A.* This is where the going gets tough. It is always hard to eliminate all the possible influences, save one, in a situation. The time-honored technique in experimental social science is to select two groups of subjects, duplicate as closely as possible everything in the environments of the two groups, and introduce the suspected causal variable to one group (the experimental group) and not the other (the control group).

A classic example of the problems that arise in using the experimental-control group technique is the "Hawthorne" experiments where one group of workers was placed in a more pleasing physical environment for their assembly-line work. This experimental group consistently outproduced the control group. The trouble was, however, that the increased productivity was later discovered to be mostly the effect of another variable—the special attention given the experimental group by the managers and experimenters themselves—rather than the physical surroundings. The experimenters had unknowingly introduced uncontrolled psychological factors: the two groups were actually operating in different environments, thus violating the experimental-control group procedure.

Most social scientists view the understanding of causation as the culmination of a long process of hypothesis formation and testing. The usual technique is to begin with a series of experiments to isolate the one variable that has the most obvious connection to the caused event. By this means, suspected sources of causation can be identified. The remaining logical steps usually demand a very high order of experimental elaboration. Consequently, beginners in the field are better off staying with relationships that can be more easily managed.

Because social science involves issues of great personal importance, it is hard to cultivate the habit of caution in hypothesis formation. Most beginners overstate their hypotheses, which leads them into measurement difficulties and the disappointments of an overworked conclusion. In trying to decide how strong a relationship to test for, give some thought to the measurements available as well as to the data resources within reach. A completely reported research experiment always contains the researcher's speculations about the larger ramifications of the results. But these are more palatable if the study itself observes sensible limits of hypothesis statement and measurement technique.

Variables

Operationalizing Variables

Early in our discussion of social scientific concepts, we saw how language begins with the problem of assigning names to different phenomena. Social scientific language consists of agreements between people that a given behavior is properly referred to by a given name. Variable operationalizing, in a way, reverses the process by which language is formed: start with the name of the phenomenon that interests you, and work backward to find ways of tying that name to the specific behavior to which it refers. To operationalize a variable means essentially to fit the name used for a behavior to some specific way of observing and measuring that behavior.

The word "operationalization" makes the process discussed here sound special and expert, when in fact it is commonplace in everyday life. I once heard an argument in a saloon over which people are better, Kentuckians or West Virginians. The "discussion" revolved around such items as the observation that one person's cousin's uncle's father-in-law was from Kentucky and he was no damn good. However, by comparison, it seems that the other person's former boss married a woman whose nephew was from West Virginia and he was born to be hanged! After several volleys of this sort, it became clear that the variables, *Kentuckians* and *West Virginians,* had been operationalized in terms of the affinity for criminal behavior of people living in those states.

As any science develops, the number of variable names that refer to carefully specified objects, events, or behaviors increases. There are now in the social sciences whole catalogues of variables operationalized in terms of specific behaviors and possible measurements.[3]

With a little luck the variables that interest you have already been operationalized in a variety of ways. Even so, you need to know a number of techniques for operationalization in order to gain analytical flexibility and to be critical of what other people have done. In addition,

---

[3] See John P. Robinson, Jerrold G. Rusk, and Kendra B. Head, *Measures of Political Attitudes* (1968); John P. Robinson, Robert Athanasiou, and Kendra B. Head, *Measures of Occupational Attitudes and Occupational Characteristics* (1969); and John P. Robinson and Phillip R. Shaver, *Measures of Social Psychological Attitudes* (1969). All are published by the Institute for Social Research of the University of Michigan, Ann Arbor.

you need to learn how to get around problems that arise when variables require forms of measurement that are outside your resources.

There are two ways of dealing with a variable that, for some reason, is not amenable to operationalization: *substitution* and *division*.

Suppose your hypothesis is: *The more educated people are, the more likely they are to be socialists.* Education isn't hard to operationalize: the number of years spent in school tells you about exposure to formal education.

Whether or not people are socialists, and if so, how socialistic they are, is quite another matter. The ideology called socialism brings together a complex of theories, versions of history, plans for action, and standards of good and bad. This bundle of things becomes all the harder to understand when it is realized that scholars of the subject have trouble agreeing on just what socialism means. Added to the difficulty of isolating a standard definition of socialism is the problem of dealing with unshared interpretations of the word on the part of the researcher, presumably trained in the formal ideological concept, and the sample survey respondent, who may think socialists are people who favor fluoridated water.

So it won't do to ask people, "Are you a socialist and, if so, how much of a socialist?" The answers to that question would generate some interesting data on self-perception, but the question would be too sloppy as a means of relating the respondent's attitudes to something as systematic as socialist philosophy. *Substituting* for the variable *socialism* might solve some of these problems. Another variable could be found that pins down the attitudes involved more directly and deals with them in concrete terms. How about: *The more educated people become, the more they favor government-financed social welfare programs.*

The advantage here is that questions can be asked on a matter most people have an opinion about, and in terms that they can relate to, such as the desirability of government financing for education, medical care, jobs for the unemployed, and a guaranteed income. However, to understand how people feel about social welfare programs is not quite the same as figuring out how socialistic they are; the government programs mentioned are not necessarily at the core of socialist ideology. It does help with the problem by picking up on an important element of socialist ideology even though it is a substitution.

Division is another way of dealing with a difficult variable. Behavior is very seldom simple; it occurs in the context of related actions, attitudes, and dispositions. Often the variables social scientists deal with can be seen as combinations of behavioral ingredients. The variable *alienation*, for example, is now frequently divided into four specific characteristics that are tied to the way people are thought to feel when they are alienated: normless, powerless, meaningless, and helpless. Attitude scales have been developed to try to measure each of those attitude ingredients of alienation. By combining measures of all four attitudes or feelings, you will have data that could respectably be said to have something to do with alienation.

Dimensions of Variables

Variables, like people, have different dimensions. A psychologist measuring personality might come up with a classification of introverted and extroverted personalities. He or she might also come up with a characterization of aggressivity-passivity on a scale from 1 to 10. These represent different dimensions of one variable: *personality.*

Public opinion is usually analyzed in terms of a variety of dimensions:

> *Direction:* The *for*-ness or *against*-ness of the opinion.
> *Location:* Where on the scale from *for* to *against* is the opinion found?
> *Intensity:* How strongly or weakly held is the opinion?
> *Stability:* How changeable is it?
> *Latency:* How close to the surface of the opinion structure is it?
> *Salience:* How important is that opinion in relation to others the person holds? [4]

All these dimensions contain different measurement possibilities, and there are a variety of techniques available to handle them. The *direction* of opinion requires only a

---

[4] Adapted from Bradlee Karan, "Public Opinion and the New Ohio Criminal Code," The College of Wooster, Symposium on Public Opinion and the New Ohio Criminal Code, July 9–30, 1973, pp. 6–8; and Vladimir Orlando Key, Jr., *Public Opinion and American Democracy* (New York: Knopf, 1961), pp. 11–18.

Key discusses variables in terms of their *properties* rather than their *dimensions.* With respect to public opinion, he uses the term "dimension" where I have used "location." In recent usage, the term "properties" has become a general name for all the characteristics of a variable: its measurements as well as its various substantive components, or dimensions, which has acquired the more specific meaning I refer to.

specification that tells whether the opinion is on the "yes" side or the "no" side. *Salience,* on the other hand, allows an ordering of opinions from no salience to very great salience. *Intensity* of opinion suggests the possibility of scaling.

Before doing much work on a variable, think over which dimension you are looking at and what the other possible dimensions might be. Select those dimensions that are most promising in getting to the core of the variable. By looking at alternative dimensions, choices can be made as to which dimensions get to the crux of the variable and which dimensions can be measured by the means available to you. At the same time, understanding the various dimensions of a variable provides perspective on what has or has not yet been done to understand the variable.

Measurement

The term "measurement" will be used rather broadly in this section. The first topic is the measurement of variables, and we will examine the levels of measurement possible for different sorts of variables. Secondly, we present some techniques for measuring the relations *between* variables. The idea is to grasp some basic tools for reducing data about two or more related variables into a statistic that characterizes the association between them. The third sort of measurement concerns the problem of specifying the significance of data obtained through scientific procedures. There are techniques for making fairly precise judgments about the chances that a set of data may simply be the result of accident or chance rather than meaningful measurement. In this connection, we show how sample surveys are constructed and the kinds of errors that enter into polling.

Conventionally, measurement as a term applies only to the first of these forms. The second is often seen as a question of characterizing the association between things, rather than of measurement, strictly speaking. The third, specifying the significance of data, utilizes probability, which isn't, in the narrowest sense, a form of measurement. Yet all three topics have to do with establishing quantities of something: the amount of variation, the degree of association between variables, and the level of significance we can attribute to data. Consequently, all three topics have been fitted under the broad rubric of measurement.

Measuring Variables: Levels of Measurement

Measurement is a deceptive subject. At first, it seems simple—measurement answers the question, "How much?" This appears easy enough to answer when talking about length or weight, but not so easy when considering such common fodder for social science as information levels, personal characteristics, feelings, and actions. The reason for the difficulty resides not so much in the matter of counting up units of things, as in the nature of the things being counted. Different variables have different possibilities when it comes to measurement.

Two considerations determine what kind of measurement can be attempted and, therefore, what sort of hypothetical relationships can be formulated using the variable. The considerations are:

1. The *properties* of the variable
2. The level of measurement *technique* available for dealing with those properties

Consider, for example, a variable such as *marital status*. The variable refers to a classification according to a legal definition: single (with the subdivisions of unmarried, divorced, widowed), or married (with, I suppose, the subdivisions of monogamous or polygamous?). In "measuring" someone's marital status the property of the variable dictates that you can't do more than categorize—it's not possible to say that someone is very much married or very little married. In the eyes of the law, you either are or are not in such a status. Given such a *property*, the variable *marital status* doesn't call for very fancy measurement *technique*.

The variable *intelligence* poses a different possibility for measurement. The *properties* of the variable do not limit consideration to classification: the variable has properties that imply larger and smaller amounts. This is where *technique* comes in. People have puzzled for centuries over how to measure intelligence. Efforts have included tests such as the sense to come in out of the rain—in which case intelligence can be measured in two categories: those who do and those who don't have the sense to come in out of the rain. Research marches on, however, and we have the IQ test. The IQ test gives us a reading on how well people can answer certain kinds of questions that are thought to have something to do with intelligence. This advance in technique permits something more than simple classification of the dull and the bright; it allows fairly detailed gradations between the low and high ends of an intelligence scale.

Measurement comprises an area of research all by itself. Researchers keep trying to develop measurement techniques that can explore all the properties of important variables. In order to systematize our understanding of various kinds of possible measurements, scientists have come up with a classification of the levels of measurement. The four levels are:

Nominal
Ordinal
Interval
Ratio

In Figure 4.1, the characteristics of these levels are explored. The *nominal* level doesn't quite seem like measurement; it refers to classifications of things. Take ethnicity for an example. If Sinnika is a Finn and Igor is a Russian, we have said something about the properties of each in relation to a variable called *ethnicity*. That's measurement, but not very fancy measurement. We can't rate Finns above Russians (except according to some other variable such as fondness for vodka—and even then, it would be close), therefore classification, or nominal measurement, is all that the properties of *ethnicity* as a variable allows.[5] Nominal measurement, low grade as it is, pops up frequently in social science as the examples listed in the figure indicate: race, region, sex, occupation, and so on.

---

[5] We could, *within* each ethnic group, identify on the basis of parentage what proportion of a person's heritage belongs to an ethnic grouping, but the notion of ethnicity itself is classificatory.

FIGURE 4.1 LEVELS OF MEASUREMENT

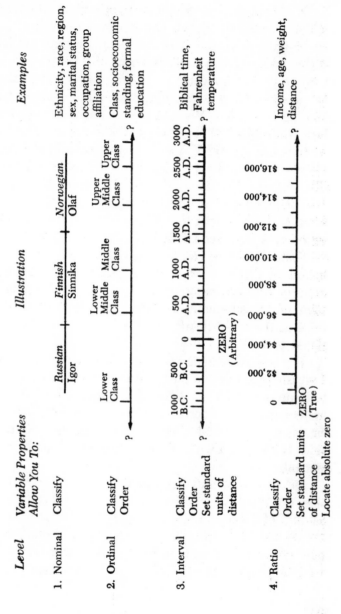

Level	Variable Properties Allow You To:	Illustration	Examples
1. Nominal	Classify		Ethnicity, race, region, sex, marital status, occupation, group affiliation
2. Ordinal	Classify Order		Class, socioeconomic standing, formal education
3. Interval	Classify Order Set standard units of distance		Biblical time, Fahrenheit temperature
4. Ratio	Classify Order Set standard units of distance Locate absolute zero		Income, age, weight, distance

If the properties of the variable allow ordering as well as classification, the *ordinal* level of measurement can be attempted, provided the techniques are available. At this level, we can think in terms of a continuum, that is, an array that indicates variation, as opposed to simple classification. Class is one illustration, and socioeconomic standing is another. We can say that Alphonse is upper class, while Mack is lower class. These are classifications, but they are arranged in such a way as to link them together on a continuum from lower to higher. Similarly with formal education: Angelina has a Ph.D., Mary a high school education, and Jane a grade school certificate. However; a Ph.D. isn't the same "distance" from a college degree as a high school diploma is from a grade school certificate. Ordering yes; standard distance no. The specification of distance or, more generally, the amount of variation between cases, is an important step up in the realm of measurement. Distance affords a decided increase in the sophistication with which a variable can be related to reality.

If standard distance can be achieved, the next level of measurement enters the picture: *interval* measurement. Here, units can be identified that indicate how far each case is from each other case. That's reasonable, but there remains one of those technicalities that causes pain to the mind. It has to do with absolute zero on a scale of measurement.

Interval measures do not have a true zero; *ratio* scales do. What is a true zero? And what good is it? In the example of biblical time, the year "zero" doesn't mean that no time has transpired in history. We don't really know where true zero is in history. Zero was established in relationship to the life of Christ for religious reasons and serves as a convenient reference point for counting forwards and backwards. The same is true of Fahrenheit temperature. You know that 0 degrees Fahrenheit doesn't represent a true zero because −23 degrees is a lot colder than 0 degrees.

A *ratio* scale like distance differs from an interval scale in that in a ratio scale zero inches means just that —no distance at all. There can't be less than zero distance, or less than zero weight, or less than zero bananas. That tells you the formal difference between a *true* zero and an *arbitrary* zero, or one that is made up for the sake of convenience.

But, what good is a true zero? The answer has to do with what can be said in comparing observations on a ratio or an interval scale. If Hardy weighs 200 pounds and Laurel weighs 100 pounds (ratio scale), we can see that Hardy is twice as heavy as Laurel. But if the temperature is 50 degrees on Monday and 25 degrees on Wednesday (interval scale), can we really say that it was twice as hot on Monday as on Wednesday? You can try and get away with it, but you really shouldn't, because a comparison of that kind requires a *true* zero. You need to know what the total absence of heat is when making out that one day was twice as hot as another. Without a beginning point, distances *can* be established, but *not* ratios.

The reason for knowing these distinctions has to do with the kind of relationships that can be established statistically within and between variables. The job is to avoid comparison of apples and oranges. Statistics enter this text only in the form of ideas behind numbers—the arithmetic and the finer points of various statistical operations are left to more advanced writings. Here we will content ourselves with a simple point (simple as statistics go). Roughly speaking:

> *Nominal* measurement allows statistics having to do with the frequency of cases in each classification.
> *Ordinal* measurement allows statistics that describe the way the cases are ordered with respect to a variable.
> *Interval* measurement permits comparisons of quantitative differences among cases on a scale.
> *Ratio* measurement permits comparisons of absolute distances between cases.[6]

Because these levels of measurement are the key to how relations between variables can be approached, it is essential to figure out the appropriate level of measurement for each variable before proceeding with research. We will see the significance of levels of measurement

---

[6] From Sidney Siegel, *Nonparametric Statistics for the Social Sciences* (New York: McGraw-Hill, 1956), p. 30. For a more recent treatment of correlation possibilities, see David Leege and Wayne Francis, *Political Research* (New York: Basic Books, 1974), pp. 287–316.

For those who know something about statistics, the following is a list of examples of statistics appropriate to each level:

Nominal: Mode, Frequency, Contingency coefficient
Ordinal: Median, Percentile, Spearman's *rho*, Kendall W, Goodman-Kruskal's *gamma*
Interval: Mean, Standard deviation, Pearson product-moment correlation, Multiple product-moment correlation
Ratio: Geometric mean, Coefficient of variation

spelled out in more detail as we turn to the problem of measuring variable relationships in the form of correlations.

Measuring Relationships Between Variables: Association and Correlation

Establishing the degree of association between two or more variables gets at the heart of the scientific enterprise. Scientists spend most of their time figuring out how one thing relates to another and structuring these relationships into explanatory theories.

As with other forms of measurement, the question of association comes up frequently in normal discourse, as in: "like father, like son"; "if you've seen one, you've seen 'em all"; "an orange a day keeps the scurvy away." In measuring the degree of association between variables statistically, scientists are merely doing what science is famous for: being rigorous and precise about a commonplace activity.

Association can sometimes be characterized in relatively simple ways. The effects of one variable on another can be described in words or by statistics. "People who use Crest have fewer cavities" is a statement that presents a relationship between an independent variable, *brushing with Crest*, and a dependent variable, *number of cavities*.

Descriptive statistics such as the median, the average, and the standard deviation can be employed effectively in specifying association. In the Lipsitz study, response scores to a questionnaire were averaged to indicate the relationship between the kind of job held and fatalistic attitudes.[7] Percentage differences are also handy comparative instruments. If 99 percent of those on the crew of the *Santa Maria* who ate an orange every day didn't get scurvy, and 60 percent of those who ate no oranges (or any other fruit) *did* get scurvy, we can say that the chances of getting scurvy were vastly reduced by regular orange-eating.

For certain applications, statisticians have developed a more sophisticated tool for specifying relationships between variables: correlation analysis.

Correlation is usually approached as a statistical matter; here we will concentrate on the ideas behind it. Our discussion should help you to know a correlation statistic when you see one. To understand the arithmetic and the limiting assumptions, you may consult a statistics text.

The essential idea of correlation is to describe statistically the association between variables. Correlation analysis is an advance over comparing percentage differences because it allows you to summarize in a single statistic both the *direction* and the *amount* of association. *Direction* refers to whether the association is positive, that is, when variable A changes, variable B changes in the same direction; or negative, if A changes, B changes in the opposite direction. The positive/negative direction is expressed by a + or − before the correlation figure. There is a positive correlation between the quantity of helium in a balloon and the rate at which it rises. There is a negative correlation between the rate of rise and the weight in the balloon.

[7] See Appendix, p. 136.

The *amount* of correlation is expressed by the size of the number on a scale from zero to +1.00 or −1.00. The scale is illustrated in Figure 4.2. Thus the correlation

FIGURE 4.2　THE SCALE OF CORRELATION

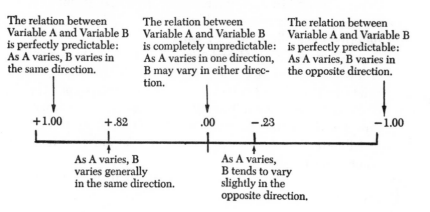

The relation between Variable A and Variable B is perfectly predictable: As A varies, B varies in the same direction.

The relation between Variable A and Variable B is completely unpredictable: As A varies in one direction, B may vary in either direction.

The relation between Variable A and Variable B is perfectly predictable: As A varies, B varies in the opposite direction.

+1.00　　+.82　　.00　　−.23　　−1.00

As A varies, B varies generally in the same direction.

As A varies, B tends to vary slightly in the opposite direction.

statistic provides a simple index of association—dangerously simple, for the mathematics behind various correlation statistics involves assumptions that require careful thought. In addition, the variety of techniques by which measures of correlation are computed causes the results to deviate slightly from the reality of the data. Understanding the general techniques by which correlation operates will allow you to see some, though not all, of the problems. Nevertheless, correlation, in the imperfect world of measurement, is a valuable tool.

The techniques for computing correlation vary with the level of measurement used. If two variables are measured on a nominal scale (classification only), there is less that can be done to characterize correlation than would be the case with two variables measured on an interval scale. In fact, there are correlation techniques available for every level of measurement, and we will describe generally how they work.

Nominal-Level Correlation Nominal measurement is low-grade stuff, and the measure of association appropriate to it barely deserves to be called correlation. The *contingency coefficient*, the statistic used here, summarizes how far the actual distribution of data deviates from a distribution in which one variable is associated with no change in the other.

Suppose some researcher wishes to reverse an old proposition and test whether or not "Blondes (unlike nonblondes) prefer gentlemen (as opposed to bums)." She interviews a random sample of twenty blondes and twenty nonblondes. If it turns out that both blondes and nonblondes have similar preferences in men, then there is nothing distinctive about the preferences of blondes and the hypothesis fails. A possible set of results illustrating the point appears in Table 4.4.

TABLE 4.4   WOMEN'S PREFERENCE IN MEN

Color of hair	Preference	
	Gentlemen	Bums
Blondes	12	8
Nonblondes	12	8

If, however, the hypothesis were correct, there would be a deviation from this kind of distribution. A statistic named the contingency coefficient computes the difference between a distribution showing *no* association of the variables and one that indicates that the variables do relate in some direction. The result is expressed as a correlation.

If, in fact, the distribution came about as shown in Table 4.5, then the contingency coefficient would be +.41.

TABLE 4.5   WOMEN'S PREFERENCE IN MEN

| Color of hair | Preference | |
	Gentlemen	Bums
Blondes	5	15
Nonblondes	14	6

The data would seem to render the hypothesis very suspect. It appears that most blondes, unlike nonblondes, prefer bums.

In more systematic language, this sort of distribution indicates some correlation between being blonde and preferring a certain type of man, in this case, bums. What has been measured by the statistic is the *deviation* from a distribution showing no difference in preferences. The contingency coefficient characterizes a pattern in the distribution of cases between two classifications. When the possibility exists of ordering as well as classifying the categories in the variable, a higher level of correlation becomes possible.

Ordinal-Level Correlation   Ordinal stands for order. It is this characteristic that supplies the basis for Spearman's rank correlation coefficient (*rho*) and other statistics that can be computed at the ordinal level. What can be done is to compare the ranking of cases according to

THE ELEMENTS OF SOCIAL SCIENTIFIC THINKING

their ordering on two variables. An illustration will help.

Imagine a group of 160 Jaycees singing "God Bless America!" The songmaster, a systematic fellow who is secretly a Marxist, rates them according to four categories of musical ability from best to worst: Canaries, Robins, Sparrows, and Crows. He wishes to test his belief that lower-class folks are better singers than the upper crust.

So he has two ordered classifications to work with: *musical ability* ordered in terms of Canaries, Robins, Sparrows, and Crows; and *class* ordered in terms of upper, upper middle, lower middle, and lower. The hypothesis he wishes to test is whether there is any association between socioeconomic class and musical ability. The songmaster hypothesizes that lower-class people sing better than upper-class people.

If that were true, the data would have a certain pattern to it. As class goes up, musical ability would go down. The lower classes would be heavily populated with Canaries, and the upper classes with Crows. Suppose he found the distribution presented in Table 4.6.

TABLE 4.6   MUSICAL ABILITY

Class	Canaries	Robins	Sparrows	Crows
Upper class	0	0	5	35
Upper-middle class	0	10	15	15
Lower-middle class	5	20	15	0
Lower class	30	10	0	0

The relationship is not crystal clear from the data, but there is a pronounced tendency for lower-class Jaycees to warble more sweetly than their "betters." We need a statistic that helps nail down the degree of association. Goodman-Kruskal's *gamma,* among other similar statistics, computes the extent to which the cases are arranged in a pattern that approximates the ordering within the variables.

Returning to the hypothesis: As we go up the class scale, does the data indicate that there is a corresponding fall off in the musical-ability scale? In the data presented in Table 4.6, the *gamma* would be −.93. Does this affirm the hypothesis? Yes. There is a negative correlation between class level and ability to sing.

Interval- and Ratio-Level Correlation To do interval or ratio measurement, you need to be able to establish distances between the units of analysis. It isn't good enough to have singers arrayed in terms of Canaries, Robins, Sparrows, and Crows; the amount of distance between Canaries and Robins and the rest has to be specified. The difference in singing ability between Canaries and Robins may be quite unlike the difference between Sparrows and Crows. With the specification of distance comes the possibility of using a correlation statistic that employs the factor of distance to measure the association between variables.

Interval and ratio measurements allow the use of a formidable-sounding statistic by the name of Pearson's product-moment correlation coefficient (Pearson's *r*).

To keep things simple, we will make up a very elementary example: the relationship in the Sheikdom of Exxit between the number of oil wells owned and number of wives. Our "sample" consists of five oil-well owners. To see what the mathematics of the Pearson's product-moment correlation accomplishes, consider two possible arrays of data. Suppose, first of all, that there is a correlation of +1.00 between number of oil wells and number of wives. Figure 4.3 illustrates sets of data for which that correlation could be claimed.

FIGURE 4.3

Number of Oil Wells

Notice the straight solid line that can be drawn connecting each case expressing the following relationship between the two variables: as oil wells increase by one, wives increase by one. A perfect correlation also results if the straight line should happen to fall on a different level; for example, see the broken line. It shows that you can get married without an oil well, but for every new wife, it appears necessary to sink a new well.

Now imagine an array of data in which the cases do *not* present themselves on a straight line. If the data were to appear as in Table 4.7 and Figure 4.4, no straight line can be drawn that connects all the cases. Pearson's *r* by a mathematical process identifies the line that most closely expresses the linear relationship. It is the one straight line

TABLE 4.7

Number of Wives	Number of Oil Wells				
	One	Two	Three	Four	Five
One		1			
Two		1			
Three				1	
Four			1		
Five					1

FIGURE 4.4

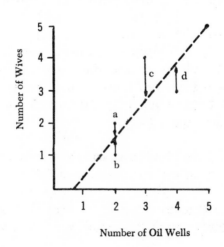

Number of Oil Wells

that is closest to all the points on the chart—the line that minimizes the distance by which all the cases deviate from the line. For mathematical reasons (best left to mathematicians), the deviations of cases from the line are measured in terms of the squares of the distances ($a^2 + b^2 + c^2 + d^2$) rather than simple distances ($a + b + c + d$). The more distance the cases are from the best-fitting line, the lower the correlation of variable A with variable B.

Notice what this procedure does *not* accomplish. A Pearson's *r* of +1.00 indicates only that any variation in A is associated with a consistent variation in B. What it does *not* tell you is the number of units B varies in relation to A. It happens in the example that as oil wells goes up by one, wives goes up by one. But if the situation were such that for *every* increase of one oil well, there is an increase of 2 wives, or ½ of a wife, or 3 wives, a +1.00 result would be obtained.

In mathematical terms, Pearson's *r* tells you only about the dispersion of cases around an imaginary straight line. It does *not* tell you the slope of the line, or, in other words, the *amount* of variation in B for every unit of variation in A. A separate statistical procedure called *regression analysis* deals with this question. Regression, however, cannot be profitably dealt with beyond this simple level, because it requires statistical concepts that are above a beginner's level.

Measuring the Significance and Representativeness of Data, Sampling, and Problems in Polling

We now turn to three topics that fit together not so much because of their general connection with measurement, but because they all relate to survey research, a major instrument of social science. To get hold of the statistical tools basic to survey research, we need to become familiar with something new: *probability.*

Probability occupies a far more important place in social science than the amount of space devoted to it in this book would suggest. Probability constitutes nothing less than a fundamental of the scientific perspective. To understand why is to come to grips with some particularly ornery habits of the human mind.

Probability refers to the likelihood or chance of something occurring. We compute probabilities about the chances of passing a course, the prospects for a date, the odds of a team winning a game. That Roget's *Thesaurus* lists so many alternatives for the word "probability"—luck, hazard, fortuity, fate, contingency, chance, and others— indicates the importance of the concept in our language.

We began by saying that science becomes useful to human beings as a way of coping with the uncertainties of life. By forcing ideas and notions out of the head and into the arena of reality and testing them, we gain knowledge about the environment. The scientific establishment is built on the psychological power provided by the effort to escape the insecurity of uncertainty about our surroundings. However, science isn't the only strategy for overcoming uncertainty about what to think. Furthermore, it is not the easiest strategy to utilize—witness the pages you have just been reading. Because scientists often couch their findings in terms of probabilities, the scientific approach often seems less satisfying than approaches that promise an easy route to certainty.

Social scientists apply probability in two special areas: determining the statistical significance of an array of data, and constructing representative samples of larger populations. Yet the objective is the same in both: trying to specify the odds that a display of data means what it appears to suggest about the relations of variables. If the information is based on a faulty sample or merely represents a chance combination of cases, then the results can't be said to tell us anything conclusive about the relationship of the variables. It is important to know that, and probability statistics provide some tools.

The first usage of probability is in establishing the likelihood of a given set of data relating two variables emerging by chance. Without probing the mathematics, we can say that a distribution of data that has a chance of occurring only one time in a hundred (a .01 level of significance) tells us something useful. The array of data very likely does say something meaningful about the relationship being measured, rather than simply reflecting a chance combination of responses. The .01 level of significance is usually considered the most acceptable, though on occasion social scientists will deal with findings that are significant at the .05 level—meaning that there are five chances (as opposed to one chance) out of a hundred of the array of data occurring by chance. The significance level of data is commonly noted as part of a research report, which helps in evaluating results.

The second application of probability relates to the way samples are selected in public opinion polling. To understand what can be done, we need to explore briefly just what sampling amounts to. In trying to summarize the behavior of large groups of people, it is seldom possible to survey all of them. Consequently, a small group is selected that hopefully represents the larger body faithfully. The degree of the representativeness is something that probability helps to indicate. Loosely stated, the question becomes: What is the probability that a given sample does not reflect the larger group from which it is drawn?

There are two general techniques used in sampling: *stratification* and *randomization*. Stratification involves trying to reproduce a large population by representing important characteristics proportionately in the sample. If we tried to determine a community's attitude toward drinking by interviewing a sample of customers at a local saloon, that sample would overrepresent one segment of the public in terms of a characteristic vital to the issue under consideration. Teetotalers don't hang out in saloons. Therefore, we would have to select the sample in such a way that teetotalers have a chance of being included. If the stratification method were used to select a sample for determining voting behavior in an election, we would try to have a sample that reflected proportionately the larger population at least in terms of class, region, and education. However, the stratification (proportionate sampling of certain categories of voters) must be limited to a relatively small number of characteristics so we do not spend valuable resources trying to find a black upper-class Jew from the South who is a Republican.

Random sampling depends on selecting at random a sufficient percentage of the population such that the chances of reproducing the essential characteristics of the total population are maximized. If we interview 5 randomly selected people out of a national population of 210 million, the chances are not so good that they are truly representative—there would be a very high margin of error. With each increase in the sampling percentage, provided the people are selected randomly, the margin of error decreases.

For any size population, it is possible to determine mathematically the probability that a given sample percentage will generate a specifiable margin of error. The margin of error drops drastically with increasing size of sample up to a point at which further increases in sample size reduce the margin of error very little. It is this point that indicates the most economical sample size. By doubling or tripling the sample size beyond this point, or even multiplying it by 10, relatively little reduction of error can be achieved.

One major problem with random sampling is that, in order to interview all of those who are randomly selected, the interviewers have to disperse their efforts and seek out respondents in all corners of the total population. Most scientific sampling uses both stratification and randomization. For example, in a national sample, one might select representative urban areas and representative rural areas (a form of stratification) and then draw a random sample within those target areas.

For their surveys of American opinion, Gallup and Harris use a stratified random sample so as to eliminate, among other problems, the inconvenience of interviewing sheepherders in the remoter sections of Nevada. The sample size is typically about 1500 persons. At this size, the margin of error is about 3 percent at the .05 level of significance. What this means is that for 95 samples out of 100, the opinions expressed by those in the sample will reflect the whole population within a range of plus or minus 3 percent. So if 49 percent of the people plan to vote for Ford for president, 95 samples out of 100 would show Ford getting somewhere between 46 percent and 52 percent of the vote if the election were held on the day of the poll. Both Gallup and Harris have a very impressive record of achievement in using samples of this kind to predict presidential elections, in part because they have been lucky in not drawing a "way-out" sample, one of the five in a hundred, and in part because they do stratify their samples somewhat to avoid the weird sample that might occur if simple random sampling were used.

It should be noted that there are other sources of error that creep into survey research besides the representativeness of the sample. A researcher may have selected a highly representative sample, however his or her instruments of measurement may elicit misleading answers. Common sources of error include those presented in Table 4.8 on p. 108.

Beyond these obvious kinds of error, there is a whole category of errors that enter in to research design; these errors arise from the difficulty of being sure you are measuring what you think you are measuring. An example would be a question developed out of an interest in understanding people's personal sympathies for the poor: Do you approve or disapprove of poor persons stealing bread when they are hungry? Someone who has enormous sympathy for the poor might say "No," because that person also has enormous respect for law and order. Note that the question is not meaningless; the error comes from attributing an inappropriate meaning to the responses. The question taps another variable, *respect for law and order*, in addition to the one intended, *attitudes toward the poor*.

Added to errors arising from sloppy measurement are errors introduced by the statistical procedures used to

TABLE 4.8

Error	Example
Ambiguous questions:	Do you think we ought to strive for peace or for a strong defense?
Symbolically loaded questions that elicit biased answers:	Do you think it is the duty of patriotic citizens to support the president of the United States in time of war?
	versus
	What do you think of President Nixon's policy on Vietnam?
Difficult questions beyond the information level of the respondent:	Do you approve or disapprove of the ballistic missile sections of the position taken by the U.S. in SALT II disarmament negotiations presently going on between the U.S. and Russia?
Response alternatives unsuited to the subject of the question:	Do you feel better or worse about the future?
Questions that include more than one issue:	Are you more likely to favor a candidate who supports busing and a strong defense or one who has a pleasing personality?

characterize the data. Statistics always distort reality to at least a small degree—that is why statisicians prefer using several techniques for characterizing data so as to hedge against the bias of a single procedure.

Conclusions

The refinements we have discussed are themselves just the beginnings of what can be done to elaborate and refine research strategies. We have sought only to map the major pathways of understanding and technique. Further development of research ability usually comes not so much from forcing down expositions of methodology as from the motivation generated by an interesting project. As the project develops, methodological matters become more significant and more rewarding to learn.

In pursuing methodological understanding, however, beware of a simple "cookbook" approach. Understand the idea of what you are doing before enlisting the specific techniques by which it can be accomplished. That, at least, is the bias of this book and the experience of this author. The wealth of detail found in the technical literature on methodology becomes much more digestible if the relatively simple ideas that underlay the calculations can be seen. Ideas provide frameworks for the mechanics of technique.

CONCEPTS INTRODUCED

Values	Direct relationship
Models	Inverse relationship
Paradigms	Causal relationship
Laws	Variable substitution
Axioms	Variable division
Pragmatism	Dimensions of variables
Induction	Properties of variables
Deduction	Measurement technique
Independent variable	Nominal
Dependent variable	Ordinal
Alternative variable	Interval
Antecedent variable	Ratio
Intervening variable	True zero
Null hypothesis	Arbitrary zero
Inferential relationship	Association
Correlative relationship	Descriptive statistics

Correlation
Direction of association
Amount of correlation
Scale of correlation
Classification
Rank order
Distance between cases

Regression analysis
Probability
Significance of data
Random sampling
Stratified sampling
Margin of error

OUTLINE

CHAPTER FIVE

REFLECTIONS:
BACK TO THE ROOTS

"The philosophers have only interpreted the world in various ways; the point, however, is to change it."

KARL MARX

Our brief study began with the very foundations of knowing: the emergence of language concepts from elementary human experience. Now the structure of method raised on this foundation can, with the aid of insights gained by our excursion into the operational side of sci-

113

ence, be addressed in a more sophisticated manner. It is time to put science itself into the perspective of a broader understanding. We need to know a little more of how science relates the self to the world outside, how scientists relate to science and, finally, how each of us can use science as a means of increasing our power to control our own environment.

Factuality, Reality, and Actuality

The scientific method often appears at first as a kind of narrow and restrictive way of reaching understanding. The demands for precision are rigorous, the statistics forbidding and, all too often, the results difficult to read. Zealous defenders of science sometimes indiscreetly claim for science more than it can support as a strategy of knowledge.

In trying to gain perspective on science, we can learn something from one of this century's major theorists of the human condition, Erik Erikson. In the course of his experience as a psychoanalyst, his research on various subcultures, and his extensive studies of crucial personalities in history, Erikson came to characterize understanding as multidimensional. Erikson distinguishes between three dimensions of our relationship to the world around us: *factuality, reality,* and *actuality.*[1] Science, as we will see, is involved with each of these dimensions.

---

[1] See Erik Erikson, *Gandhi's Truth* (New York: Norton, 1969), p. 396; *Dimensions of a New Identity* (New York: Norton, 1974), pp. 33–34; and *Life History and the Historical Moment* (New York: Norton, 1975), pp. 103–104. Erikson's formulations of these concepts vary somewhat and I have adapted them to suit the purposes of this exposition.

Of the three, *factuality* fits most closely with the popular view of scientific methodology. *Factuality is that "universe of facts, data, and techniques that can be verified with the observational methods and the work techniques of the time."* [2]

Much of what we have been considering here deals with the effort to establish that elusive item of inquiry, the fact. Earlier I hinted at a personal dislike for the word "fact." By now, however, enough has been said to make it clear that facts are not to be confused with Truth. A fact is only as good as the means of verification used to establish it. A great deal of science consists of using methodological advances to revise, modify, or even falsify "facts" and theories formerly "verified" by cruder or less sensitive techniques. By trying to verify observations systematically, we strengthen the bridge between our perceptions of the world and phenomena outside ourselves.

All the concern with thoughtful variable specification, precise measurement, and the cautious interpretation of results has to do both with developing data worthy of being called factual and with understanding the limits of such data. While the factual view of the world seldom seems to have the glamour or subtlety of, say, the poetic view, we have tried to establish that it has a power and social utility of its own. Factuality is a necessary component of our world view, though the limitations on creating factual information, and the human characteristics we bring to the task, require a broader perspective on knowledge.

Reality, the second of the dimensions, or aspects, of

---

[2] Erikson, *Dimensions of a New Identity,* p. 33, italics mine.

understanding, is somewhat less concrete, but perhaps intuitively quite simple. Our sense of what constitutes reality is not merely a summation of factuality. *What we know as reality is, rather, a perspective on factuality integrated by the sense in which we understand these things.* Given the limitations of fact-gathering technique, the pressures of the moment, and the unconscious elements in the background of our understanding, we have to be aware that, no matter how hard we try, our understanding will never be exclusively factual. Nor need it be. Science is a discipline for finding and organizing evidence about what interests us. We then try to use that evidence to shape our view of reality. Consequently, we can legitimately ask of those who do science that they convey to us not just the "facts," but something of their perspective on the realities reflected in their data.

A science that is to be social must engage in a kind of balancing act between the scientific principle that statements must be verified and the social necessity for doing something about the crises of civilization. Verification of social theory often lags behind the necessities of social policy. In bringing together the verified and the speculative through an insightful sense of reality, we increase the possibility of social progress. Developing this kind of approach to reality is no simple matter, nor can we say exactly how it comes about—except that personal commitment, experience, a willingness to suspend preconceived ideas, and good scientific procedure all play a part.

Factuality, the world of data and observation, and a sense of reality, the perspective in which we understand evidence, do not yet comprise the whole of knowledge. Erikson suggests a third dimension of existence, *actuality,* which for our purposes means *knowledge gained in and through action.* Science creates an image of reflective inquiry, of the researcher observing phenomena to gather information and then retreating to some quiet place to assemble, digest, and characterize what can be known. Yet such a detached mode of understanding is not typical of most of us. Human beings are, after all, more oriented to action than reflection. Actuality has something to do with how we act on (or transact between) the modes of our knowing and the occasions for behavior.

Erikson illustrates his concept of actuality by discussing his own experience as a psychoanalyst. Psychoanalysis is basically a highly developed form of behavioral inquiry. Erikson comments that therapy is never really a process by which a doctor prescribes some course of action to a patient, but rather a *mutual* exploration to which the psychoanalyst brings training and experience, and the patient a personal history, deep feelings, and capacities for insight and action. The psychoanalytic encounter matches *potentialities* between doctor and patient. The same can be said for social scientific inquiry. The behavior we study does not simply lie there on a slide plate or bubble in a test tube; it is formed out of the same animating principles that move the researcher as a person. The best social scientists are those who become engaged by the behavior they study. They use rigorous analysis, but they also reach into action itself as a source of understanding.

Social scientists are very circumspect about the question of personal involvement in the behavior they study. The obvious reason is that disciplined thought can be hard enough to achieve, without intruding the feelings evoked by becoming engaged. Yet all social inquiry consists of a personal transaction with something outside ourselves. As a personal stance, remoteness has its dis-

117

advantages just as involvement does. Whatever strategy is adopted, good inquiry really calls for a very high level of consciousness. The scientific method makes conscious and explicit that part of the transaction dealing with the verification of observations. There is a similar need to be highly conscious of how one's own experience and personality enter into the task of understanding.[3]

Aside from forcing a recognition of the personal elements of inquiry, Erikson suggests that experiential involvement opens up potentialities for insight. Behavior is reflexive; it emerges through transactions with an environment. Understanding the transactions possible in an environment requires a "feel" for what is human about behavior. Such understanding demands an appreciation of factuality and a perspective on reality, but also a sense of action and what it can reveal.

Every student has gone through the process of learning something intellectually and then relearning it through experience. Science is recommended as that mode of knowing that will most benefit one's ability to establish facts, understand the reality surrounding them, and approach actuality with sensitivity.

[3] Some classics of social science owe their particular value to the personal involvement of the authors in their subject matter; for example, Floyd Hunter, *Community Power Structure* (New York: Doubleday, 1963); Robert Lane, *Political Ideology: Why the American Common Man Believes What He Does* (New York: Free Press, 1962); C. Wright Mills, *The Power Elite* (New York: Oxford University Press, 1959); William Whyte, *Street Corner Society* (Chicago: University of Chicago Press, 1943).

Of Scientists, Science, and Paradigms

Science is practiced by people, not machines. Or, more accurately, science is practiced by groups of people. The major fields of social scientific inquiry are dominated by communities of scientists, usually located at major research institutions, and tied together by a network of journals, conferences, and procedures for mutual evaluation and discussion.[4] While substantial disagreements often exist within these scholarly communities, there is usually a rough consensus about the boundaries of the principal problems, the standards by which they can be dealt with, and the values that must inform the recommendations. No one in the American social scientific community, for example, writes about the desirability of dictatorial government. And, until recently, very few scholars would consider seriously an openly Marxist approach to the understanding of social and political conflict.

The fact that there are communities of people involved in the enterprise of social science introduces a number of considerations that need to be reckoned with in evaluating social scientific research. First of all, few of us really like being unique or different from everyone else.

---

[4] An intriguing discussion of the history of science that details the role of scientific communities in structuring understanding is Thomas Kuhn's *The Structure of Scientific Revolutions*, 2nd ed. (Chicago: University of Chicago Press, 1970), on which some of these themes are based.

Nor do people particularly enjoy having to face large problems from a point of view entirely their own. By this I mean that there is a natural psychological pressure toward conformity in all human activity, as well as in scientific inquiry.

Several factors reinforce this tendency toward conformity. One such factor is the career structure of the major disciplines. Though invisible to most students, careers in academic institutions typically hinge on a kind of master-apprentice system. Those who study with the famous master receive the best positions and the greatest access to means of communicating their views. Ability assuredly has a great deal to do with who gets close to the master and how successfully he or she manages to parlay this position into a reputable scholarly career. But the net effect of this system is a significant pressure for the perpetuation of established viewpoints, since the apprentice frequently identifies with the position of his or her master.

To this pressure for conformity, add yet another factor: the political significance of social scientific research. Researchers who probe elements of corruption in the economic system or in social welfare agencies, for example, are not likely to enjoy the favor of their targets. Even the investigation of socioeconomic power as it enters into community decision-making quickly becomes controversial. Since schools and institutions are usually run by trustees who represent dominant interests, there can be career risks in certain kinds of research projects.

Another factor influencing conformity with safer forms of social explanation is that research costs money. Survey research, upon which much good social science depends, costs a lot of money and usually requires financing from governmental agencies, businesses, or foundations.

The kind of professional who attracts this money is not likely to be too far out of touch with prevailing social and political ideas.

For these reasons, scientific inquiry is frequently characterized by schools of thought or paradigms that structure the way problems are defined and solved. Yet, in the face of all these pressures, the ultimate virtue of the scientific method, as opposed to other forms of inquiry, is that the steps by which knowledge is gathered are public and open to inspection and challenge. The point of reciting the factors that prejudice inquiry is not to discredit science, since most of these factors operate in other forms of inquiry as well, but rather to emphasize yet another reason for being critical of accepted knowledge and scientific in your own standards of evaluation. One of the first questions to ask on reading any book, taking any course, or selecting any field of research should be: What is the dominant paradigm behind this form of inquiry? Once these are understood, you are in a position to evaluate evidence carefully.

The Radicalism of Science

After what has been said about the conformist tendencies of the scientific establishment, even allowing for the brief message of reconsideration at the end, it may seem perverse to start talking about the radicalism of science. So be it; not all has yet been said on the subject. Science can be radical in a social sense and a personal sense as well.

Scientific inquiry began as a revolt against dogma established and controlled by dominant political and religious institutions. The history of science is filled with cases

121

of intrepid analysts who emerged from their laboratories with findings that threatened prevailing understandings in all fields of human inquiry. Some scientists have paid even with their lives for such heresies. The control of information is one of the fundamentals of political power. Scientists, by insisting on reasonably open and accountable procedures of information-gathering and conclusion formation, have slowly begun to chip away at the power of those who would foreclose inquiry in favor of pet theories and self-serving doctrines.

More relevant to daily life are the ways in which a scientific habit of mind can contribute to your own ability to resist conditioning and deal knowledgeably with your environment. We are all bombarded daily with arguments to do this or that based on somebody else's conception of what is good and bad. For most people most of the time, estimations of the credibility of sources suffice to separate the smart advice from the nonsense. But it doesn't hurt to have a means of independent evaluation.

Western culture has for a long time viewed social problems as a matter of the weakness of human nature. This approach invites introspection and the examination of personal intentions, motives, and dispositions. Social science, by and large, encourages a different approach: look around you. Before deciding that the individual is totally responsible for his or her actions, consider the environmental factors, the structures of power, the forces of conditioning, the real dimensions of choice that face people in social situations, and the material possibilities people actually have of solving their own problems. These circumstances are sometimes more susceptible to change than are inward dispositions that grow out of a conscious and unconscious history of individual development.

Science enters into personal action as a method for disciplining the process of understanding experience. The safeguards of the scientific method exist principally to control the natural tendency to project on what is observed whatever we want the world to be for our own private purposes. A discipline it is, but it becomes in practice a method of personal liberation from the narrowness of our own views, the limits of our powers of observation, and the pressures of our prejudices. Science, a discipline all may develop, can become a radical force in a world that badly needs to be changed.

CONCEPTS INTRODUCED

Factuality
Reality
Actuality
Scientific community

Career structures
Conformist social explanation
Scientific radicalism

APPENDIX

WORK LIFE AND POLITICAL ATTITUDES: A STUDY OF MANUAL WORKERS *

LEWIS LIPSITZ
University of North Carolina

For centuries men have speculated about the human consequences of work. Slowly, a considerable body of information has

* I want to thank Charles Walker and Chris Argyris of Yale University, Robert Guest of Dartmouth, Edward Gray of the United Automobile Workers, and the officers and members of UAW Local 595 for their criticism and suggestions. A special debt is owed Robert Lane of Yale whose work helped stimulate this study and whose disagreements with the author aided considerably in the task of clarification.

SOURCE: Reprinted by permission from the *American Political Science Review*, Vol. 58, No. 4 (December 1964), pp. 951–962.

begun to accumulate concerning the relationships between people's jobs and other aspects of their lives. Investigators have pointed out the connections between certain types of jobs and certain personality disorders, job satisfaction, productivity, attitudes toward union and management, social relations on the job, leisure activities, and other things.[1] Extending such findings, this study concludes that a particular job situation can have important effects on a man's political outlook.

Political studies have long classified individuals according to occupation, yet there have been extremely few efforts to penetrate within specific occupational categories to discover the causal triggers of occupational attitude differences. Political scientists have, on the whole, been content to work with relatively large groupings such as "semi-skilled" manual workers, "unskilled" manual workers, etc. Several efforts have been made, however, in the direction this study takes; exploring specific job characteristics and their effects on political attitudes. Seymour Lipset cites a work that established a relation between size of factory and voting Communist or Nazi in pre-Hitler Germany. William Kornhauser observes the connection between the rate of expansion of a particular industry in the early stages of industrialization and the political ideology of the

---

[1] See in particular Georges Friedmann, *Industrial Society: The Emergence of the Human Problems of Automation,* trans. Harold L. Sheppard (Glencoe, 1955), p. 276; Robert Blauner, "Work Satisfaction and Industrial Trends in Modern Society," *Labor and Trade Unionism: an Interdisciplinary Reader,* ed. Walter Galenson and Seymour Martin Lipset (New York, 1960), pp. 339–360; E. L. Trist and K. W. Bamforth, "Some Social and Psychological Consequences of the Longwall Method of Coal-getting," *Human Relations,* Vol. 4 (1951), pp. 3–38; Charles R. Walker and Robert Guest, *The Man on the Assembly Line* (Cambridge, Harvard University Press, 1952); Frank J. Jasinski, "Technological Delimitation of Reciprocal Relationships: A Study of Interaction Patterns in Industry," *Human Organization,* Vol. 15 (1956), pp. 24–28; David Armstrong, "Meaning in Work," *New Left Review,* No. 10 (July–August, 1961), pp. 16–23; and Georges Friedmann, *The Anatomy of Work—Labor, Leisure and the Implications of Automation,* trans. Wyatt Rawson (New York, 1961), p. 107.

emerging labor movement.[2] In such findings, we move somewhat closer to establishing a causal relationship between something about a particular work situation and certain attitudes or behavior of the job holders.

But more specifically, concerning the problem of job satisfaction, Lipset, writing in 1960 observed that it was yet to be shown that "job satisfaction and creativity contribute independently to political behavior over and beyond differences in status and economic conditions. . . . "[3] The present study indicates that a particular work situation, that of the automobile assembly-line, affects the political and social attitudes of the automobile workers involved. The ways in which the concrete work situation affects the worker's political attitudes are determined by the technology and social setting of the job itself. Specifically, assembly-line workers are found to be more fatalistic, more punitive, and more politically radical than other workers of comparable salary and education who work in the same plant.

I

Before proceeding to the findings themselves, it may be helpful first to consider briefly the nature of assembly-line work, in comparison with other occupational types.

The social and psychological consequences of work have been much debated. The factory is a symbol of modern life, and the assembly-line in particular has often been thought to embody in extreme form the worst tendencies of industrial work. Other analysts have argued, to the contrary, that modern industrial societies offer more individuals more chances for genuine work satisfaction than any previous societies.[4] It would serve little purpose here to get involved in this controversy, for even if the issues raised remain unresolved, certain facts about modern work-life relevant to

---

[2] Lipset, "The Psychology of Voting," *Handbook of Social Psychology*, ed. Gardner Lindzey (Cambridge, Addison-Wesley, 1954), II, 1139; Kornhauser, *The Politics of Mass Society* (Glencoe, 1959), p. 154.

[3] *Political Man* (Garden City, N.Y., 1960), p. 237.

[4] Blauner, *loc. cit.*

our inquiry are quite clear. First, manual workers generally indicate lower work satisfaction than non-manual workers. Second, within the manual group, satisfaction varies with skill: the higher the skill, other things being equal, the greater the satisfaction. The table below provides some frame of reference for dealing with the question of job satisfaction in manual and non-manual jobs.

TABLE I. PROPORTION IN VARIOUS OCCUPATIONS WHO WOULD CHOOSE SAME KIND OF WORK IF BEGINNING CAREER AGAIN [5]

Professional Occupations	%	Working Class Occupations	%
Mathematicians	91	Skilled printers	52
Physicists	89	Paper workers	52
Biologists	89	Skilled automobile workers	41
Chemists	86	Skilled steelworkers	41
Lawyers	83	Textile workers	31
Journalists	82	Unskilled steelworkers	21
		Unskilled automobile workers	16

Beyond the question of how workers respond when asked if they are satisfied with their jobs, a more important question concerns the *effects* of work; what impact the job has on a man's life outside of the factory. Many writers and analysts have speculated about this. Much of the analysis of industrial work emphasizes its destructive or negative aspects and focuses attention on the elimination of skill and the increase of simple, repetitive, assembly-line style work. Yet, there have been only a few studies of assembly-line jobs.

The development of the assembly-line was part of what one

[5] *Ibid.*, p. 343. The extent of satisfaction expressed is clearly in part a function of the particular question asked. For example, a group of American unskilled workers asked "Are you satisfied or dissatisfied with your present job?" showed 72% indicating they were satisfied. Exactly what satisfaction means in such a case is not at all clear. See Alex Inkeles, "Industrial Man: The Relation of Status to Experience, Perception and Value," *American Journal of Sociology*, Vol. 66 (July, 1960), p. 6.

observer has called the "second industrial revolution." Although overhead conveyors were emloyed from the 1870s on in the American packinghouse industry, they were not introduced on a large scale until 1914, when Ford's Highland Park, Michigan plant became conveyor equipped. After 1920, assembly-lines were rapidly adopted in many areas of heavy industry.

Charles Walker and Robert Guest, who made probably the most thorough study of assembly-line work, characterized the "pure" assembly-line job as involving the following six elements: [6]

1. Mechanical pacing of work
2. Repetitiveness
3. Minimum skill requirement
4. No choice in the use of tools or techniques
5. Minute subdivision of the product worked on
6. The need for constant surface attention.

The expectation that men would dislike assembly-line work is borne out by current research. Consistently, investigators have found that conveyor-paced jobs in mass production industries show lower levels of satisfaction than other manual and non-manual jobs. Blauner concludes that assembly-line work is more disliked than any other major type of work.[7] Within the automobile industry, which is the setting of this study, the position of the semi-skilled line worker is difficult. Possibilities of advancement within the ranks are extremely slim. Wage differentials between the highest and lowest paid production jobs are small.[8]

Automobile assembly-line workers have little control over the pacing of work. The average worker on the line performs no more than five operations, remains at his station at all times, and repeats the same operations about 40 times an hour. For most workers, the

---

[6] Walker and Guest, *loc. cit.*, p. 19.

[7] Blauner, *loc. cit.*, pp. 346–347.

[8] Arthur N. Turner, "Impersonality and Group Membership: A Case Study of an Automobile Assembly Line" (unpublished Ph.D. dissertation, Cornell University, 1958), pp. 13–16.

work cycle is between one and two minutes, regulated by the conveyor speed.

Characteristically, the assembly-line worker is alone on his job. The technology of the line increases the worker's sense of impersonality and presents barriers to group cohesiveness. Moreover, there appears to be no adjustment to the assembly-line as time passes. The longer a man has held an assembly-line job, the more likely he is to have an unfavorable attitude toward all aspects of work experience.[9]

What do we know about the effects of assembly-line work? Compared to other groups of manual workers, assembly-line workers show few grievances, little use of pressure tactics, and much internal disunity and evidence of suppressed discontent. They permit leadership to gravitate to aggressive individuals with a strong need to dominate. They accept certain elements of their work life as inevitable, and they lack self-confidence.[10]

When Walker and Guest compared workers holding "pure" assembly-line jobs with another group of workers whose jobs were more skilled, varied and autonomous, they found that absenteeism was much higher on repetitive, conveyor-paced jobs; repetitiveness was negatively correlated with interest in work; limitations on talking were a source of frustration to line workers; mass production methods tend to increase the worker's sense of anonymity.[11] My study indicates that the differences Sayles and Walker and Guest find between different groups of semi-skilled factory workers carry over into the area of political attitudes.

II

Three samples of workers were used here as the basis for comparisons:

1. assembly-line workers, or men with jobs approximating those of the assembly-line

---

[9] *Ibid.*, p. 26.
[10] Leonard Sayles, *Behavior of Industrial Work Groups: Prediction and Control* (New York, 1958).
[11] Walker and Guest, *loc. cit.*

2. repair, relief, and utility workers
3. skilled maintenance workers.

Repair, relief and utility workers were chosen as the semi-skilled group for purposes of comparison because their jobs provided them with greater autonomy and variety than the line workers had. Repair jobs, for example, could not be time-studied and were not completely repetitive. Individual judgment and some choice of tools were required. Relief and utility workers both performed as stand-ins for men along the assembly-line, but were competent to handle many kinds of line jobs within a given department of the shop. Their work was more varied and likely to lead to a stronger sense of pride and a deeper interest in the task.

The repair, relief and utility workers, like the assembly-line operatives, would normally be classified as semi-skilled in a social class or occupational breakdown.[12] Skilled workers were also included since they would furnish an important comparison with both semi-skilled groups and might exhibit in greater detail or more extensive development tendencies found in the other groups.

Names were selected at random from the files of the local union. Men willing to participate were interviewed in their homes. The interview questions were almost entirely open-ended. In addition to the interviews, each man completed a questionnaire which incorporated various attitude scales and other questions. All of the men interviewed were married, native-born, and white. The three groups were closely comparable in many respects. Educationally, all three groups averaged between nine and ten years of education completed. A majority of each group was Catholic. The mean age of each sample was between 40 and 50. Assembly-line workers interviewed had been on their present jobs an average of six years; repair workers, twelve years; and skilled workers, thirteen years. Pay rates in the two semi-skilled groups varied between $2.40 and

[12] See, for example, the classifications employed by Albert J. Reiss, Jr., in "Change in the Occupational Structure of the United States, 1910–1950," *Cities and Society, The Revised Reader in Urban Sociology,* ed. Paul K. Hatt and Albert J. Reiss (New York, 1957), pp. 424–431.

$2.74 an hour, while in the skilled group the rates ranged from $2.96 to $3.39.

The assembly plant in which these men worked was located in Linden, New Jersey. At the time of these interviews, between 2900 and 3000 men were employed at the plant. The general effort was to study intensively the political orientations of a relatively small group of men, to gain some insights of general applicability that could then be tested on a larger sample, more systematically.

III

The three work groups showed attitude differences in five areas: the job; the union; a fatalistic view of social life; the extent of preoccupations with economic problems; and the extent of sympathy and tolerance.

The Job. Assembly-line workers view their jobs with a mixture of anger and resignation. Almost all of them complain bitterly of overwork, physical strain, and monotony. They feel subjected to undue pressures because of the excessive speed of the line, but they feel powerless to control this speed. Relationships with supervisors are marked by inequality and anxiety. These men feel expendable. They know there is nothing unique about their performances at work.

All the repair, relief and utility workers have ambivalent attitudes toward their jobs. Many complain of pressure and overwork, of physical and emotional strain. Yet they also note compensating factors: variety, skill, and the very important fact that the men on the assembly-line have much more unpleasant jobs than theirs.

The fifteen skilled workers present a picture of their jobs in extremely vivid contrast to those offered by the other two groups. Not a single man dislikes his job, and the degree of satisfaction is high in most cases. By and large, these men note as important the fact that they set their own pace of work; they are not closely supervised. They speak of pleasure in the creative use of their skills. They feel themselves in a position to perform useful and appreciated services for others. They have relatively good relations with supervisors. They show no sense of resignation to the inevitable; they know they can leave the corporation since they possess skills needed elsewhere. They have a certain self-confidence built on the knowledge that they have something valuable to sell.

The following tables will convey some notion of the differences in job attitudes among the three groups.

TABLE II. MAJOR COMPLAINTS ABOUT JOB

	Per cent citing					
Occupation	Pressure or overwork	Physical or mental strain	No skill or monotony	Bad supervision	Exploitation	N
Line	75	50	75	58	50	12
Repair	50	43	7	36	43	14
Skilled	13	13	0	20	7	15

TABLE III. MAJOR SOURCES OF JOB SATISFACTION

	Per cent citing					
Occupation	Variety or skill	Good supervision	Autonomy on Job	Better than line	Any kind of satisfaction	N
Line	0	0	0	0	42	12
Repair	78	28	0	57	78	14
Skilled	80	67	27	67	100	15

The Union. The twelve line workers show slightly favorable attitudes toward unions. Only four are altogether favorable. Five others are ambivalent, citing both good and bad features of unionism. Finally, three men are largely hostile toward unions.

TABLE IV. ATTITUDE TOWARD LEAVING PRESENT JOB

Occupation	% Who would leave if possible	% Who feel stuck	N
Line	91	75	12
Repair	71	64	14
Skilled	27	13	15

Those with anything good to say about unions note "protection" as the most important union function; indeed, it is the one positive union function the line workers cite. They see the union as the only force that blunts the exploiting bent of the company. Several of the men mention seniority as an especially important kind of protection. Those who criticize the union concentrate their attention on the idea that unions are not controlled by the workers but rather by a clique which serves its own interests. They assert unions are corrupt and uninterested in the rank-and-file. As a group, these men are not closely attached to their union. They give no indication of a sense of participation or solidarity.

The views of the repair, relief and utility workers resemble those of the line workers in several respects, but differ in several others. These workers show more favorable feelings toward unions generally and also toward their own union. Eight of the fourteen men have pro-union attitudes, while six are ambivalent. None is completely anti-union. Like the line workers, they stress the importance of "protection" as a union function, but four of the men also note union benefits such as vacations, company-paid insurance, etc. Within the repair group, only one man accuses unions of being oligarchical. Criticisms move in other directions and seem to be less intensely felt than among the line workers.

Much as might be expected, the skilled maintenance men also show relatively favorable attitudes toward unions. Seven are wholly pro-union, while the eight others are ambivalent. This group, too, emphasizes the "protection" the union offers, but stresses union benefits even more than the other groups. None of these skilled workers show the sense of abandonment found in the line sample. And none of them criticize unions as oligarchies.

Attitudes toward Walter Reuther, President of the United Auto Workers, are quite revealing. Both the line and repair workers are sharply critical of their union head. A majority in both groups condemns Reuther as a man out for himself, personally ambitious, and uninterested in the fate of the ordinary worker. Even men who praise the UAW as a whole, and unions generally, are wholly negative where Reuther is concerned. The skilled workers, by contrast, are overwhelmingly favorable toward Reuther; praise his skill and intelligence, as well as his honesty and dedication. In all, attitudes toward Reuther are more extreme (both positive and negative) than attitudes toward unions generally, or the UAW in particular. The line workers, who are most unhappy at work, are least happy with unions and with Reuther. The skilled workers, who are most satisfied on the job, are largely pleased with unions and with Reuther. The repair group occupies a middle position in both areas.

TABLE V. OVERALL ATTITUDE TOWARD UNIONS

	% Generally favorable	% Pro-UAW critical of others	% Ambiv- alent	% Generally unfavorable	N
Line	33	0	42	25	12
Repair	28.5	28.5	43	0	14
Skilled	46	0	54	0	15

TABLE VI. ATTITUDES TOWARD WALTER REUTHER

	% Favorable or ambivalent	% Unfavorable	N
Line	25	75	12
Repair	36	64	14
Skilled	86	14	15

Fatalistic Attitudes. It is sometimes argued that fatalistic attitudes do not characterize industrial man. Fatalism, it is held, is characteristic of the peasantry, lending support to rigid class distinctions and to the idea that the political order is not to be tampered with.[13]

No doubt citizens of industrial societies are not as fatalistic

[13] See Daniel Lerner, *The Passing of Traditional Society: Modernizing the Middle East* (Glencoe, 1958); and David Riesman, Nathan Glazer, and Reuel Denny, *The Lonely Crowd: A Study of the Changing American Character* (New Haven, Yale University Press, 1950).

as their ancestors. Yet it is also clear that the social and technical structures of industrial societies themselves produce certain fatalistic orientations, and that these are related to the specific kinds of work men are engaged in. Those workers who are conscious of having the least control over their own lives at work show the most pronounced tendency to view the social and political worlds as unalterable.

To say the very least, it is difficult to determine the degree of fatalism comprised in an individual's outlook. In an effort to find an approximate means of measurement, individuals were scored on a fatalism scale composed of four open-ended interview questions. The table below indicates the results of this scoring.

TABLE VII. FATALISM SCORES BY JOB GROUPS *

Occu-pation	Number of Fatalistic Answers					Mean score
	None	One	Two	Three	Four	
Line	0	2	3	5	2	2.58
Repair	3	2	5	2	2	1.86
Skilled	3	6	3	3	0	1.40

* The four questions that made up the scale were:
1. Will men and nations always fight wars with one another?
2. Will there always be poverty in the world?
3. Do you think the ordinary man is helpless to change some aspect of government he doesn't like, or is there something he can do about it?
4. Some people say they can plan ahead for long-range goals and then carry out their plans. Others say, "Whatever's going to be is going to be and there's no sense planning." How do you feel about it?

The four questions form a Guttmann-type scale with a reproducibility coefficient of .91, and a minimal marginal reproducibility of .671. Analysis of Variance significant at .05
t Test for Line and Repair significant at .15
t Test for Line and Skilled significant at .01

There are clear differences among the three work groups and these differences are in the expected direction. The assembly-line workers are the most strongly fatalistic. Though there is not space here to explore the types and nuances of fatalistic attitudes, a few important points need to be made. First, as a group, these men are most strongly fatalistic about the problem of war. The idea of the inevitability of aggression fits well with the picture these men have of human nature. Second, fatalistic attitudes are weakest in the area of the political potency of the ordinary citizen. These men retain the notion that a letter to one's congressman will change things. They hold to this idea despite the fact that on other questions they indicate their belief that public officials don't really care about the common person.[14]

The non-fatalistic workers in the sample stand out most strongly from their fatalistic fellows in two respects. First, they are indignant rather than merely sullen and resigned about conditions they find unacceptable. Second, the non-fatalists tend to blame themselves as well as others for social failures. They emphasize the possible triumph of justice, even if only in the distant future, and the possibility of humane and rational behavior, even though many of them consider such behavior unlikely.

Economic Preoccupations and Political Radicalism. The assembly-line group is more politically radical than the other two samples of workers. This manifests itself in favorable attitudes toward governmental economic controls and antagonisms toward private ownership and the privileged orders; it is closely related to a strong tendency among the line workers to emphasize economic problems and interpretations.

The distribution of attitudes along the liberal-conservative continuum is in the expected direction. The assembly-line workers are the most radical, the skilled workers the least. The patterns for the three groups bear a close resemblance to the scores for skilled, semi-skilled manual workers which Centers found in a nationwide sample in the late 1940's.

Symptomatic of their economic preoccupations, two contrasts

---

[14] Generally speaking, these findings confirm previous ideas about working class political attitudes in the United States. For a discussion of the pessimism of working class attitudes on international affairs, see Gabriel A. Almond, *The American People and Foreign Policy* (New York, 1950), pp. 123–130.

TABLE VIII. WORK GROUP SCORES ON
LIBERALISM-CONSERVATISM SCALE [15]

	% Ultra-conser-vative	% Conser-vative	% Inde-termi-nate	% Radical	% Ultra-radical	N
Line	0	8	33	42	17	12
Repair	8	15	54	23	0	13
Skilled	13	33	27	20	7	15

X^2—.10

emerge among the work groups in which the line workers attach a greater emphasis to economic considerations. First, they tend more strongly to view economic problems as the most important ones confronting America today. Fifty-eight per cent of the line group ranks economic problems most important as compared with 36 per cent of the repair group and 33 per cent of the skilled workers.

The kinds of economic problems mentioned by the different groups were also quite distinct. All of the men in the assembly-line group who mentioned economic problems at all concerned themselves either with unemployment or poor working conditions; both problems very close to home. In contrast, men in the other two groups raised questions about high taxes, foreign aid, welfare excesses, salary differentials, and the demise of free enterprise.

Second, the concern with economic difficulties shows itself in

[15] The Liberalism-Conservatism Scale is taken from Richard Centers' book *The Psychology of Social Classes* (Princeton, Princeton University Press, 1949). The scale was part of the questionnaire administered with each interview. One man in the repair category never completed this questionnaire and so only 13, instead of 14 men are scored above. The Centers scale basically compares 19th century liberalism (conservative) with 20th century liberalism (radical—welfare state). The questions explore management versus labor identification; belief in the possibilities of economic opportunity; attitude toward government ownership and social insurance.

responses to a question that asks about the nature of the "chains" men feel. The question was phrased, "A man once said: 'Man is born free, but everywhere he is in chains.' Does this mean anything to you?" Table IX arranges the responses according to whether the

TABLE IX. RESPONSES TO ROUSSEAU

	% Offering economic interpretation	% Offering non-economic interpretation	N *
Line	86	14	7
Repair	77	23	13
Skilled	27	73	11

* Percentages are based only on those who offered some interpretation and therefore exclude the "don't knows."
$X^2 = .02$

individual saw Rousseau's "chains" in economic terms.

Table IX is significant not only because the line and repair workers tend to perceive "chains" in economic terms, but also because they tend to see these "chains" as oppressive. Remisik, a repairman, typifies much of the commentary: ". . . has to earn his bread. He's chained to a job of some sort, regardless of whether it's here or any other concern. . . ." The "chains" these men see range over bills, the regimentation of factory life, and the income tax. On the other hand, most of those who offer non-economic interpretations think of "chains" without the element of oppression. Harris, a maintenance painter, serves as a good example: "Yeah, everybody is born free, true—but then we acquire chains. It has to be. There's law, regulations that we have to abide by. . . . We're always in chains, but chains can get awfully heavy in some of these countries."

Sympathy and Tolerance. None of the questions in the interview schedule was designed directly to explore dimensions of sympathy or tolerance. Yet, several of the questions seemed to elicit punitive responses from some of the men but not from others. All of these questions touched on attitudes toward "out-groups." The four questions were:

1. Why are people poor?
2. What should our policy be toward Russia?
3. Do you think it was a good idea to drop atomic bombs on Japan in World War II?
4. How do you feel about capital punishment?

Though the evidence is very skimpy and impressionistic, it appears that the assembly-line group is less sympathetic and tolerant than the others. In all of the four cases, the line workers are slightly more punitive as a group. They tend more strongly to blame the poor themselves for poverty. They were more likely to approve the bombing of Japan without showing any sympathy for the Japanese, and to recommend a policy of toughness toward Russia. Finally, they were somewhat more likely to favor the death penalty.

These findings are worth noting largely because they tend to confirm previous conclusions about authoritarianism and social class. Within this group of workers, punitive attitudes are associated with work frustration and lack of control over worklife. These facts point up the possible significance of everyday frustrations in conditioning attitudes toward outgroups.[16] The possibility that such frustrations might play an important role in shaping attitudes is one that psycho-analytic research has left open for the moment.[17]

IV

In two important areas the three groups show attitudes that are much alike but are important to describe nonetheless in order to give greater definition to the picture of working class views

[16] Lipset points out that the unemployed, feeling resentful and alienated, are less tolerant of minority groups than are employed workers, a finding that seems related to the conclusions here about the assembly-line group. See S. M. Lipset, *Political Man: The Social Bases of Politics* (Garden City, 1960), p. 114. For a discussion of the importance of attitudes toward out-groups, see T. W. Adorno and associates, *The Authoritarian Personality* (New York, 1950), chs. 2–4.

[17] See Bjorn Christiansen, *Attitudes Towards Foreign Affairs as a Function of Personality* (Oslo, Norway, Oslo University Press, 1959), p. 59.

drawn thus far. First, a majority of the men in all three groups emphasize the manipulative nature of much of social life. They express concern about the exploiting and unfair practices of their corporation and of big business generally. Moreover, approximately half the men express concern about two-faced, deliberately deceptive tactics of the government and mass media which they see as closely related. Table X shows the distribution of such attitudes in the three work groups.

TABLE X. PER CENT PERCEIVING MANIPULATIVE
PRACTICES BY BIG BUSINESS OR CORPORATION
X, AND BY GOVERNMENT OR MASS MEDIA *

	See manip. by Corp. X or big business	See manip. by govt. or mass media	N
	(%)	(%)	
Line	92	50	12
Repair	79	43	14
Skilled	60	47	15

* The specific questions asked were:
1. How do you feel about big business?
2. How do you feel about Corporation X?
3. Do you feel there's much corruption in politics? Why?

Where big business is concerned, these workers see manipulative practices everywhere. A few believe big business or the rich run the United States. Others are not quite so explicit, but believe that big business is free of the restraints that bind ordinary mortals: businesses can initiate wars, bribe judges and representatives and manage to get the government to follow their dictates. In some of these men, hostile attitudes toward big business and especially toward their own corporation, attain a frenzied pitch and a deep bitterness.

Most of the men feel that the corporation acts as it does because its primary concern is profit-making. Some see businesses caught in a competitive rat-race in which it is do or die. The methods of the rich, as these workers describe them, are not subtle. These men simply affirm the idea that "money talks." Very few of them have any praise for big business. Most simply accept it as a fact of life, unable, like the line worker Tencio, to visualize a world without it: "Well, without big business, what could the working man do? He gotta work for big business."

It is not particularly surprising to learn that many of these working class men are critical of big business. But it is very much another thing to find that almost half of the 41 men are critical of manipulative and deceptive aspects of American government and the mass media. The chief theme of the critics is that the government is immune to popular pressures. The general picture is of a group of men who arrange to keep themselves in power and who don't care about the requests of the common people. The means of governmental manipulation are varied: nepotism, misleading propaganda, suppression of information, bribery, silencing of dissent. The credibility of the media is to some degree tied up with the credibility of the government. Several of the men feel that the radio, papers, television only convey what they are told to. They are tools, willing or unwilling, of the politicians. Five men criticize the media as manipulative in their own right. All who discuss the media do so in terms of their deceptive political content.

Some of the workers who are concerned about manipulations tend in the direction of a conspiracy theory of social control. Yet few of them actually express anything resembling a theory of a hidden oligarchy or oligarchies. At most, seven men give any clear indications of holding to such a picture of American society. In all seven cases, it is the "rich," or "big business" which is said to be the ruling elite.

The remaining two-thirds of the men who criticize various manipulative practices give no indication of adhering to a power-elite theory. They criticize business, government and media for attempting to manipulate the common man, but their criticism is specific and piecemeal. They do not have any clearly formulated picture of social life, nor any precise notions about who is to blame for the seamy side of things. They are critical of the excessive power of big business and yet do not believe that big business runs the country. They can believe that people in the government attempt to mislead the public without going sour on government as a whole.

Yet, behind their vagueness and their sense of their own ignorance, most of these men actually have developed an explanation for the practices they criticize. First, they see a society directed toward profit-making. Second, they are aware of wide disparities of power. Out of these elements, these men have constructed a suspicion of human nature. It is human nature and nothing less, they say, which leads to the malpractices of business and government. Thus, it is not a particular group of evil men who are to blame, but rather the selfishness supposedly inherent in almost all of us.[18]

These workers generally accept the profit-motive as a satisfactory explanation of business behavior. But this does not account for governmental behavior. Why these failures, large and small, in the democratic system?

A substantial majority of the men believe that politics, like most other aspects of our society, is basically a business. Three-quarters of the line workers, 57 per cent of the repair sample, and 60 per cent of the maintenance men see politicians as predominantly self-seeking. They see elections and platforms designed to fool the public; politicians seeking to perpetuate their own domination; stealing, nepotism, the wasting of public funds, etc. A government composed of such individuals could not possibly be very attentive to the kinds of problems these workers are concerned about. It is not surprising then that they see failures in the political system. The selfish nature of politicians springs from their unfortunate and seemingly indelible humanity.

The second important area of similarity among the three groups is political participation. Unexpectedly, all three groups were strikingly alike in regard to voting, discussion of politics, and

[18] Thus, most of these men are not "cabalists" as that term is used by Robert E. Lane. Describing the cabalist frame of mind Lane notes: (1) There is some unofficial, quasi-conspiratorial group behind the scenes to manipulate and control public affairs; (2) each cabal group is responsible to no one but itself, and (3) the cabalist argument is protean; for the same person it will focus now upon the international banker and now upon the Communists. . . .
Lane argues that such a pattern of thought is rooted both in personality weaknesses and the social processes of modern society. He finds this frame of mind among men with anti-democratic tendencies. See his *Political Ideology*, ch. 7.

interest in political affairs. A majority of the men in all three groups reported talking politics at least sometimes. Only one man indicated he was not interested in presidential elections. Only a handful felt that the outcome of the 1960 presidential election made no difference. All of the men said they had voted in 1960.

Only in two areas did any tentative difference appear among the three work groups. First, the skilled workers were more likely than the other groups to participate in political activities beyond voting. Two-thirds of the skilled group had contributed money, gone to party meetings or actively campaigned in recent years. In the repair group, the figure was 43 per cent, and in the line group, 36 per cent.

Second, the quality of partisan commitment varies considerably among these groups. Very crudely, there are two sorts of commitment: positive and negative—being in favor of, or being against. Most notably, the line workers phrase their political commitments in terms of their aversion for the Republican Party as well as their preference for the Democrats. Five of the twelve line workers speak of their ill-feeling toward the GOP. This ill-feeling runs the gamut from quiet discontent to raw bitterness. Dolski, a line worker, speaks with particular resentment on the subject of poverty: "Why do we have poor people in this state? I'll tell you: Republicans got in there. They kept everything for themselves. Now we got the poor in. . . ."

V

Much of the evidence set out in the preceding sections is impressionistic and statistically insignificant. Yet the weight of the evidence points in a single direction.

It is clear that the two groups of semi-skilled auto workers hold different views in various areas of life. First, the men who work on repetitive, assembly-line jobs dislike their work more and are more hostile toward and alienated from the union. Second, the assembly-line workers are more fatalistic, less sympathetic with and tolerant of others. The line workers are also more radical in their political views.

Recent investigations of Arthur Kornhauser tend to confirm

these findings. In an as yet unpublished work and in a recent article, Kornhauser explores the relationships between skill level and various psychological and attitude variables. He finds that skill level in manual jobs is clearly related to mental health and also to certain political and social attitudes. He concludes that the higher the skill level of the job, the more likely that men will show high mental health, while mental health is lowest among workers with repetitive conveyor-paced jobs.[19]

Kornhauser's measures of mental health coincide, in part, with dimensions of attitudes also examined in this study. His indices include measures of: anxiety and tension; hostility *versus* trust in people; self-esteem *versus* negative self-feelings; sociability *versus* withdrawal; personal morale *versus* anomie or social alienation. He also found, consistent with the findings here, that workers in lower skill jobs were higher on economic "liberalism," but lower in liberal attitudes on race relations and international affairs. Kornhauser concludes that the workers at various skill levels differ most sharply

[19] Arthur Kornhauser, "The Mental Health of the Industrial Worker—A Detroit Study" (preliminary draft, August, 1962); "Mental Health of Factory Workers: A Detroit Study," *Human Organization*, Vol. 21 (1962), pp. 43–46. The following table (*ibid.*, p. 45), will indicate his findings:

MENTAL HEALTH OF FACTORY WORKERS

Men in 40s (age)	% With good mental health scores	N
Skilled	56	45
High Semi-Skilled	41	98
Ordinary SS	38	82
Repetitive SS	26	73
Repetitive machine-paced only (subdivision of preceding category)	16	32

These relationships held when the author controlled for education.

in feelings of defeat, pessimism, personal inadequacy, futility, and distrust of others.[20]

Assembly-line workers, as we have seen, do not find their work interesting. They complain bitterly and consistently about monotony. In many respects, automobile assembly-line work reflects the most unhealthy characteristics of industrial work. Line workers have a sense of futility. They are frustrated and at the same time are seeking to undo their sense of inadequacy. Their frustrations are clearly reflected in their alienation, *i.e.*, their feelings of powerlessness, and its attendant consequences. Their feelings of helplessness are reflected in their fatalistic acceptance of their lot and of the agonies of the great world. Their efforts to restore their self-esteem are reflected in their desires for economic improvement.[21]

What are the implications of these findings for our understanding of political life?

First, it seems reasonable to suppose that assembly-line workers and others whose jobs deprive them of control over their physical movements are more likely to sympathize with radical and mass agitations. Assembly-line workers are more isolated and more likely to feel disenfranchised than other industrial workers. Their feelings about politics are likely to be influenced by desires for relatively radical change, even if these feelings are partly suppressed.

---

[20] Though I have spoken of a causal relationship between jobs and attitudes, I have not really "proven" such a relationship exists. The crucial problem is one of pre-selection. Perhaps men on assembly-line jobs differ from other semi-skilled workers because they were different before they ever took these jobs, rather than because they have been changed by their employment. Perhaps it is only men with a low sense of self-esteem and strong withdrawal tendencies who stay on the assembly-line. Kornhauser tries to handle this problem by exploring the life of his interviewees before they took their present jobs. He concludes that there is demonstrable evidence that jobs change attitudes, regardless of what those attitudes were before the job was taken. If so, then personality differences that exist before taking the job do not explain occupational group differences in mental health. See "Mental Health of Factory Workers," *loc. cit.*, p. 46.

[21] Demands for justice and self-esteem can take many forms. For a discussion see Denis Butt, "Workers' Control," *New Left Review*, No. 10 (July–August 1961), pp. 24–33.

Second, it seems clear that the job structure of industry is one factor that needs to be understood in grasping the impact of industrialization. Kornhauser has pointed out that it is not industrialization *per se*, but rather "discontinuities" in industrial development that have been the basis for antidemocratic movements.[22] Among these discontinuities are excessive rapidity of industrialization or the acute breakdown of the economy. Perhaps along with these factors we should also turn our attention to the job structure of emerging industries, focusing on the proportion of assembly-line type jobs.

Third, specific job groups may show a clearer relationship to political party allegiance in countries with multi-party systems than they seem to in America. The great majority of workers in all of the sample groups examined here were Democrats, yet the groups differed in the extent to which they favored liberal economic measures, and in the intensity of their antagonism to the Republicans. In a country where a greater variety of political choices is offered, such differences within the strata of manual workers may show up more sharply in party allegiances. And conversely, if most of the men in most circumstances vote Democratic anyway, regardless of differences in their feelings, party organizers here may well be content to get them to the polls and ignore their feelings.

Finally, how widely can these findings be generalized? If recent work in industrial psychology is any indication, a large percentage of manual and white collar workers are not interested in their work. It seems as yet an open question whether interest in work and control over work will increase or decrease with the spread of various forms of automation. At any rate, millions, if not tens of millions of Americans in the foreseeable future are likely to be working at uninteresting, repetitive jobs. Perhaps such workers, even if they are not manual workers, will internalize the tensions and dissatisfactions of their work.

I am not attempting to argue that a bored clerk in a department store, a dish-washer in a restaurant, an auto assembly worker, and an IBM card puncher are likely to respond to their jobs in

---

[22] Kornhauser, *The Politics of Mass Society, op. cit.*

147

the same manner. Their political and social attitudes are conditioned by the content and status of their jobs, as well as the circumstances and expectations they bring with them, and other factors. Yet it seems possible that at each status level, those with the most repetitive, least interesting or controllable jobs will be the most dissatisfied, alienated, and politically "radical." [23]

VI

Various political analysts have argued that there is a causal connection between industrialization and democracy. Among the most prominent of these probably is Lipset, who has shown correlations between stable democratic systems and various indices which provide a way of measuring the relative modernity of nations.[24] In his view, contradicting Marx, industrialization tends to produce the preconditions for political democracy because the class struggle is shaped in moderate directions. Relative wealth and increased education tend to preclude extremism in the lower classes. The absence of deep and stable class differences also makes it possible for the rich and privileged to acknowledge the poor as members of the same species.

Robert Lane has recently buttressed Lipset's argument from another direction. His research, in depth interviews, of the attitudes of a sample of "common men" in an Eastern city reveals that the work situation in which these men find themselves is conducive to the formation of democratic norms. Most of his sample have substantial independence at work, find satisfaction in their jobs, exercise some skill, are in a position to assert their competence and to exchange views with co-workers and superiors. Lane's findings also move in the direction of substantiating Blauner's hypothesis that modern industrial work provides wider opportunities for the

[23] There is an extreme divergence of views concerning the composition of the manual workforce. For example, compare the emphasis in the appendix to Friedmann's *Anatomy of Work—Labor, Leisure and the Implications of Automation*, trans. Wyatt Rawson (New York, 1961), with the notes to Blauner, *loc. cit.*

[24] "Some Social Requisites of Democracy," this REVIEW, Vol. 53 (March 1959), pp. 69–105; see also his *Political Man, op. cit.*, ch. 2.

exercise of skill than work in previous societies. Lane concludes that the data on industrial work substantiate Lipset's correlation between democracy and advanced industrial development.[25]

The findings reported here, as well as those of Kornhauser noted above, are not nearly so so optimistic as Lane's or Blauner's. It seems that at some lower skill levels work alienation is considerable, and has serious psychological and political consequences, some of which are not very healthy for a democratic polity. On the basis of the very incomplete knowledge we have about the effects of different types of work, skepticism about the overall consequences of industrial work is still in order.

The manual workers examined in this study are not extremists in the sense of favoring truly radical change, revolution, violence, or of lending support to undemocratic political movements. But it is not their jobs, at least in the case of the two groups of semi-skilled workers, that have made them supporters of the *status quo*, nor taught them very much about the nature of democratic social relationships. If these men are defenders of the political *status quo* it seems to be largely because of their status as consumers, not because of their work lives. If they have very much sense of personal adequacy, it is because of the control and judgment they are able to exercise outside their jobs. Though industrial work, for many reasons, may be more conducive to the development of democratic sentiments than the life of the peasant, it is quite another thing to argue that industrial work, at least of the repetitive variety, is generally healthy or enhances an individual's sense of worth.

Lipset's argument concerning the relationship between industrialization and democracy seems to run counter to the analyses of writers such as C. Wright Mills and Erich Fromm. Fromm and Mills emphasize the alienation and apathy characteristic of bureaucratized industrial societies.[26] They argue that democracy is far from being

[25] *Political Ideology*, ch. 15.

[26] Mills' point of view is set out in *White Collar, The American Middle Classes* (New York, Oxford Univ. Press, 1951); *The Power Elite* (New York, Oxford Univ. Press, 1959), and *The Causes of World War III* (New York, 1960). Fromm's views can be found, in part, in *The Sane Society* (New York, 1955).

a reality in today's world. As they picture it, many ordinary citizens have become passive and alienated, feel unable to control their fates, and have lost sight of the significant issues of political life. Both Mills and Fromm relate these characteristics of industrial societies to the structure of work. Both argue that alienation and passivity at work breed alienation and passivity elsewhere. If they are right and industrialization creates many kinds of work situations which are not conducive to the development of democratic attitudes, then how can industralization and democracy be related?

A great part of the difficulty in resolving this antithesis may lie in definitions and points of view. Lipset's definition of democracy is an arbitrary, operational one. He speaks of two characteristics: competitive parties and the absence of strong anti-democratic political groups.[27] It is a "democracy" fitting this definition which Lipset finds related to his indices of modernity. Both Fromm and Mills speak of democracy and democratic attitudes in a different sense. Both bring normative judgments to bear on present reality. So, it is possible to agree that Lipset's correlation is correct and important, and yet to agree with Mills and Fromm that present-day democracies are not as democratic as they might be.

Robert Lane has argued that ego strength is a crucial psychological correlate of democracy. Without having experienced an inner sense of mastery as well as a sense of mastery over the environment, men do not develop the requisite ego strength to pursue a consistent, long-term course, or to effect much social change. One of the most important, if unproven, implications of this study is that the work men do can have important consequences for their ego strength. Here the concerns of Fromm and Mills are significant. Men in a work environment they cannot control may be to some unknown degree damaged in their sense of mastery, and this damage may render them less capable of coping with and altering an environment they find unsatisfactory. To the extent that such damage occurs, men become victims rather than creators. To the extent that work life contributes to such incapacities, it needs im-

[27] *Political Man,* p. 48.

provement in modern societies. Industrial democracy may yet prove to be a prerequisite to political and social democracy.

A few final *caveats:* first, the severe dissatisfactions found among automobile assembly-line workers are probably not typical of the attitudes of most modern industrial workers. The nature of the assembly-line itself intensifies the problems of a mechanized job. These findings therefore represent only one segment of the working class. Their relevance to men in other types of jobs which are less intensely disliked remains to be seen.[28] Second, the findings presented in the tables above are for the most part based on a rather crude dichotomizing of attitudes as these attitudes appeared in the setting of open-ended interviews. Such findings, especially in view of the small size of the sample, are at best suggestive and exploratory. Most important, the question of the intensity with which various attitudes are held must remain moot in many of the areas this article has explored. For example, though many of the men criticize what they consider to be manipulative practices by political figures, most of them are not "alienated" from the political system. How deep their cynicism may go on occasion, is a question this study has not touched.[29]

[28] For a comparison of "alienation" in several quite different industrial settings, see Robert Blauner, *Alienation and Freedom* (Chicago, 1964).

[29] Allen Schick provides a perceptive discussion of the need to deal realistically with the presence of ambivalent political attitudes in his paper, "Alienation and Politics," delivered at the 1964 American Political Science Association convention.

INDEX